identity:

Discover your Authority in Christ

By:
Rev. Gene Herndon

"The Word is Eternal" Isaiah 40:8

Printed in the United States of America

Published by Aion Multimedia
20118 N 67th Ave
Suite 300-446
Glendale AZ 85308
www.aionmultimedia.com

Table of Contents

Chapter One: Power of Attorney

The book of Ephesians is often referred to as a blueprint for Christian and church maturity. The epistle of Paul to the Ephesian church is essential for the Christian to understand and realize his or her authority and ability in God. As a Christian, you must know who you really are. Ephesians delves into clarifying who you, as a believer, are positionally. In other words, how you *sit* in Christ as you stand and walk; how you *walk* out your relationship with Christ and how you *stand* against the attack of the enemy. The epistle is only six chapters long, and I would encourage you to read and reread it often. I happen to pray prayers every day out of the book of Ephesians and I ask that God would open the eyes of my spiritual understanding that I may be enlightened to know the glory of His riches and the hope of His calling. I ask that every day because the eyes of my understanding need to be enlightened in order for me to know the things that God has for me. If God did not enlighten us, we would walk around ignorant of his ways.

Ephesians 6:12

Ephesians 6:12 says, "For we wrestle not against flesh and blood, but against principalities, against powers, against rulers of the darkness of this world, against spiritual wickedness in high places." It is important to understand that we do not wrestle against flesh and blood. What does that mean? You do not wrestle against the people around you. Sometimes an attack can come from the person sitting next to you, someone you love. It might be a child, a parent, a spouse. Sometimes a spiritual attack seems to come from that person but the originator is really not that individual. When someone offends you, or you get offended, you pick up offense from the person not realizing that it was Satan who waged the war. You may feel like punching the person in the nose, that is, you want to "wrestle against flesh and blood." Our human tendency is such that we want to deal with offenders carnally, not realizing that the attack that is coming through them is not of their flesh and blood. It is spiritual.

Is God the only ruler of the world? That is a trick question. He says, "For we wrestle not against flesh and blood but against principalities" — in other words, earthly political governments — "against powers, against rulers of the darkness of this world and against spiritual wickedness in high places."

"Rulers of this world" — what do this mean? Isn't God the ruler of this world? In the book of Revelation, its author, the Apostle John, talks about Babylon and the world's system and that the world's system will come to an end. And he tells his children to come out of the world's system, because if they are of God then they are not of the world.

A system of governments and principalities does exist. Do you wonder why some banks, credit card companies, government, and insurance companies are corrupt and appear to have zero social conscience? Stop praying that they won't cheat and deal corruptly with the public anymore; you are praying against the Bible! Pray that God would open your eyes for you to see it clearly, respond to it correctly, take your authority over it, and not participate in it! Because He says come out of it; it is supposed fall, and eventually be destroyed. The economy is supposed to do what it is doing! It has been prophesied that there shall come a time where God will be God! This world has worshiped materialism, but it has not worshiped the true God! People have prospered and thought, "God is blessing me!" But it may not have been God who was blessing them; more likely it was the world's system (or Babylon) that was blessing them. That's why certain people prosper excessively, and appear to have all the material stuff and wealth of this life.

Nothing God gives can any man take away from you. So why are people losing stuff if God gave it to them? God said, "I open doors that no man can shut and I close doors that no man can open!" If God was the author of it, then how come their stuff keeps getting stolen? Because some things didn't come from God, and people have allowed them to become idols in their lives, and because Satan flat out steals from people.

Ephesians 6:12 ends with, "wickedness in high places." Paul said in 2 Corinthians 12:2 that he knew "a man caught up in the third heaven; such a man did not know whether he was in the body or out of the body." Paul said, "He was caught up to the third heaven." Paul was talking about himself when he said, "I couldn't tell whether I was still here or not here." He means, "All I know is I was caught up into the third heaven." Paul says he heard things that were not lawful for a man to utter. He heard the throne of God; he was not just hearing the Holy Spirit speaking to him, but he was present before the throne of God! He said, "I heard things that are not even lawful for me to speak."

If he was in the *third* heaven, it follows logic that if there is the third of something then there must be the second and the first, yes? Okay. So the first heaven is the atmosphere, that's where the airplanes and birds fly. When the Bible says "the heavenlies," sometimes it's talking about the sky, the stars, the heavenly places in relation to the earth's atmosphere and beyond.

The second heaven is the place of spiritual activity. It's where spiritual war is happening. Remember the story of Jacob's ladder from Genesis 28? It says that Jacob saw angels descending and ascending on the ladder. They were literally going up and down delivering commands and communicating messages. Generations later, the prophet Daniel refers to the same spiritual system in Daniel 10-12 when he describes his vision of angels and the one clothed in linen saying, "I heard you while you were yet speaking, but the Prince of Persia held us up." In other words, the spiritual wickedness that was happening in that second realm was interfering with the transmission between heaven, the first realm, the Earth, and the third realm, which is God's throne. The heavenly messenger said that angels were dispatched the moment Daniel opened his mouth! But the Prince of Persia was holding them up so they were late getting to him because they had to fight in the heavenlies.

As another example, I believe that if some churches moved to the Midwest, they would triple in attendance. Some areas have a "hard" heaven; because of the lack of exposure to Christ, it is very difficult for the gospel to penetrate. This explains why some people want to live their lives the way they want to, and they don't want to submit to the will of God and to the plan of God. They would rather go to the movies than come to church. If this same hardened church were uprooted and replanted in the Midwest where communities are already predisposed toward the gospel, they would draw a greater crowd.

If there are rulers in this realm and that realm is stronger in certain parts of the world than others, then their influence is more obvious in certain place. Take San Francisco, for example. You will see a spirit of homosexuality stronger there than you will see other places. Go to Las Vegas, where people are standing on the corners handing out souvenirs and flyers with naked people on them! Some areas and territories are more demonically influenced than others, so their main, most notorious problems are not because of flesh and blood; they are because of principalities, governments that have been set up and established on this planet that are devoid of God and the will of God. So their establishment is also against the people of God, and thereby against you, the Christian believer. If you would renounce your Christianity (and I'm obviously not suggesting that), most of you would remove all of your problems! Because Satan does not resist those who are in league with him!

2 Corinthians 10:4

For the sake of those who are legalistic or may be tempted to take what I say out of context, I am not telling anyone to renounce Christianity. But I do believe that the person who gives up the fight and walks away from his or her faith would find that many problems would likely go away, because that is all Satan wants believers to do. The problem is, you would be going to hell for doing that. And let me be honest with you, okay? I would rather endure, because the Bible tells me that weeping may endure for a night, but joy cometh in the morning! I would rather endure for this situation, to live 80, 90 or 100 years on this planet than to live my eternity in hell.

According to 2 Corinthians 10:4, "the weapons of our warfare are not carnal, but mighty through God to the pulling down of strongholds." We have the ability to "cast down imaginations and every..." what?

"High thing"!

"Coming from..." where?

"High places." Remember I just said high places — second heaven. That means there are thoughts that can enter your mind that did not come from God. It came from where? High places! Paul has said, basically, "The ability for you to fight your war and your battle lies in beginning to cast down all of those thoughts that come from high places because not everything is from God!" And furthermore, "If you want to overcome, part of the weapons of your warfare are your ability to recognize and discern what has come from a high place and cast it down." And he also said, "The weapons of our warfare are not carnal but mighty..." through whom? Through God! Mighty through God.

There are two New Testament words most often used to represent "the power." The same two Greek words were used to mean "mighty" or "might." One is ENERGIA or some variation thereof; ENERGIA is where we get our English word *energy*. It means the manifestation of power. The other Greek word is DUNAMIS or one of its variations, which is where we get our word *dynamite*. It means having inherent power. So if I have a stick of dynamite and I hold it in my hand, will it explode? If I light it, and then I throw it, will we clear any area? Why? Because it is going to release energy, right? So if you see the word "dunamis" or any variation thereof, it speaks to the inherent ability of something. If you see the word "energia," it speaks to the manifested power of a thing. In other words, when I throw it and it explodes, that is energy.

The word used here in 2 Corinthians 10:4 is "dunamis," which implies that Paul means that the spiritual weapons of your warfare have *inherent power* through God. So when people try to resist situations in the flesh, and they try to fix their problems in the flesh, their efforts are futile, because they cannot deal with spiritual problems by natural means! You must understand that if you're dealing with spiritual issues, you must deal with them spiritually! If you don't engage in battle through God and the weapons He provides for you, then you have no power! The only power you will have comes through God.

Luke 10:19-20

Here Jesus is speaking to the 72 disciples whom He appointed and sent out ahead of Him. He tells them, "Behold I give unto you power to tread on serpents and scorpions and over all the power of the enemy. And nothing shall by any means hurt you. Notwithstanding, in this rejoice, not that the spirits are subject unto you, but rather rejoice because your names are written in heaven." Note that He said, "I give unto you power to tread on *serpents and scorpions*." By serpents and scorpions He does not literally mean serpents and scorpions. I have seen stories of people dancing with snakes in their church and if the snake bites someone and that person dies, then that proves the person's sinfulness. Unfortunately, this portion of Scripture is being misinterpreted, which is why a student of the Word must rightly divide it. Sometimes people read these graphic sayings of Jesus and get confused because they wonder, "What does that mean?" Here in this Scripture, serpents and scorpions refer to *devils and demons*. That's why it says, "Behold I have given unto you. ..." If you are a born-again believer, you can say, "Jesus has given me power to tread over serpents and scorpions and over all the power of the enemy and nothing shall by any means hurt me."

Sometimes people use language that doesn't really convey the finality of something. So in case His disciples still didn't understand, Jesus added, " ... and by no means shall anything hurt you." Not a thing! Not some things, not a few things, but nothing shall hurt you!

Jesus begins with "I have given you power. ..." Now this is where most people miss it. That word for "power" is not DUNAMIS, or ability; it is EXOUSIA. *Exousia* means "authority." He is really saying, "I have given you authority over all the 'dunamis' [inherent ability, power] of Satan." So in other words, it is not physical strength that Jesus has given His followers.

You might hear people say, "Oh, I was travailing in the spirit!" Listen, if God told you to do that, then do it. But if you are just doing that out of the flesh, you're trying to fight your way through it, then what you are doing is fighting carnally. God did not give you the power to deal with it, and your power becomes mighty only through God! Some people get too far out there and experience defeat, and their first response is, "Well this stuff doesn't work!" No, it works if you work it properly.

There is a difference between authority and power. Imagine if I go out into the middle of the street as a semi-trailer truck is coming at me, and I stand there and I yell, "Stop!" If he has enough traction to stop before he hits me, the driver may stop the truck. But there is more of a likelihood that it will end poorly for me. However, if I pull up in my Highway Patrol car, turn my flashing lights on, and stand out with my badge on, he is going to stop. Now he is not stopping because of me, but he is stopping because of what I represent. That's the difference between authority and power.

In certain parts of Asia, people use elephants as work animals the way farmers in other parts of the world might use oxen. When the elephant is a baby, they will tie it to a tree. And the elephant calf can't break free from the tree, no matter how much the young animal pulls. It fights and tugs until all of a sudden it just stops, it gives up, it is broken. When that elephant becomes an adult, its handlers will take a rope and just lay it on the ground and tie the elephant to it, and that huge beast will stay right there! It will not move! It has power but is unaware of it because of conditioning.

Some people in the body of Christ suffer a plight similar to this elephant's. Satan has roped them to stuff, and they have fought and fought because they want to see some spiritual reality come to pass because they thought God was in it. And they have been fighting and fighting and fighting until suddenly they have given up. At that point Satan cuts the rope and lets it hang because he knows that person won't even try anymore. They won't even fight anymore. Now Satan has exercised his authority over that Christian.

The believer who doesn't know the power he has in Christ will never execute it. This is how a big elephant tied to a tree that he could literally rip out of the ground if he used his trunk will remain imprisoned, because he won't try to set himself free. He gave up trying a long time ago. That elephant has bought into the idea that greater is that tree. If we as Christians have all the power and the authority over Satan's power and ability, then the only way that we are going to be able to walk in that power and authority is to know we have it.

Years ago, when I was struggling financially, one day I was looking for money, struggling, and I opened my jewelry box and sitting on the top of it was a 100-dollar bill. I don't remember putting it there. I may have, but I can't for the life of me figure out why every time I opened my jewelry box I would not have seen it.

Here is my point: I was struggling probably for a week, not knowing that 100 dollars was in that box. So all of the struggling and all the concern and all the wrestling and all the toil and the prayer and the turmoil that I went through was for nothing! Because the reality was that in that box was what I needed in order to overcome! But because I did not know it was there, I suffered unnecessarily, not knowing that I had a supply that would resolve my issue. Because I was not aware of it, I did not know I could tap into it. I suffered for days, needlessly trying to hurry up to get to work to get home to not use my gas. I made all these adjustments in my life because I was thinking, "I don't have more," when the reality was I had it and didn't know it.

So authority is delegated power. If I leave for the day and I tell someone, "You're in charge," I have now delegated my power and my authority to that person. Whatever that person says in my name goes. If people do not do what that person tells them to do, then they will have to deal with me.

Ephesians 1:3

"Blessed be the God and Father of our Lord Jesus Christ who (will?) bless us with all spiritual blessing in heavenly places." Read it again. "Blessed be the God and Father of our Lord Jesus Christ who (someday by-and-by will?) bless us"? No! It reads, "Hath blessed us!" *Hath* is past tense. That means, that God has already blessed us with all spiritual blessing in heavenly places "according as He has chosen us in Him, through God, before the foundation of the world that we should be holy and without blame before Him in love. Having predestinated us unto the adoption of the children by Jesus Christ to Himself according to the good pleasure of His will to the praise of the glory of His grace wherein He made us, hath made us accepted in the beloved." So you have already been given all spiritual blessing! So if it is sitting in your jewelry box and you have forgotten that all spiritual blessing has been given unto you, then you will never know that all spiritual blessing has been given unto you through God, in Christ! All spiritual blessing has been given unto you for He has predestinated you before the foundation of the world that you would be where you are right now! He already knew what you were about to go through! He already knew the problems you were going to face! He already knew what you were going to struggle with and He has already predestinated you with His power in Christ! We respond with "God, do you know what I'm going through?" Yes, He knows! So if you have been blessed with all spiritual blessing, then you have been empowered by God to prosper in everything that you put your hands to.

11

2 Corinthians 5:18

I want to drive home this understanding that if you have something, then you have to know that it is yours and that it belongs to you. Every person in this world has been saved. Everybody! So you have that one person in your family who sits at home and will not go to church and does not believe in God — that person is saved. John 3:16 says, "God so loved the world," not just Christians, the world, "that He gave His only begotten Son so that whosoever shall believe on Him shall not perish but have everlasting life." Emphasis on *whosoever*.

The qualifying factor is not that they are saved, it's that they know they are saved. 2 Corinthians 17-19 says, "Therefore, if any man being in Christ is a new creature, old things are passed away, behold, all things become new. And all things are of God who hath reconciled us to Himself by Jesus Christ and have given to us the ministry of reconciliation, to wit that God was in Christ, reconciling the world unto Himself, not imputing their trespasses unto them. And He hath committed unto us the word of reconciliation." Notice here it says "the world" not just Christians.

What does that mean? That means the gospel is the good news. The good news of what? That your sins have been forgiven you. And so unto the world, He has already reconciled them back to Him! What He is giving us the ministry of is to go tell them, "You have $100 sitting in your jewelry box! You don't have to be sick, you don't have to be poor, you don't have to be in trouble, you don't have to be in despair because there is One who came to help in your time of need! Here's the good news — Jesus Christ and Him crucified! The good news!"

We have been given the Word to tell them that they have been reconciled and that their sins are no long imputed unto them! By their confession that they understand that, they are now what we call "Born again and saved." But they were saved 2,000 years ago. All we are supposed to do is tell them, "Hey! There's a box! In this box is everything you need!" See, if you don't know, you can't walk in it, can you?

Some people say, "How could God let people go to hell?" The answer is that He is not letting people go to hell; they are saved! He did his part! God has appointed us to go forth and preach the gospel to those who do not know! I knew that was what I am supposed to do! Before I was even a pastor I understood that if I was sitting in a chair in a church than every member there is a minister! There are some people who know it is their job to go forth and tell people, "You have been saved! There is One greater than me! My feet are not worthy to fill his shoes, but His name is Jesus Christ, and if you would trust Him and love Him, He will change everything in your life!"

Some people go to church just to warm a chair. The chairs don't need warming; there are people in your life who are going to hell. You need to say something; even if you don't know what to say, you can say, "Listen, Sunday morning, guess where we are going? Are you gonna come with me?" And take them to church. Ecclesiastes 3:11 tells us that God has placed eternity in the hearts of all men. In every soul lie the desire and the question of purpose and eternity. Thereby it is our only responsibility to avail them of the knowledge that they have been saved for a purpose.

God has already blessed us with all spiritual blessing. Then we already have the ability to walk in that blessing. The word *blessed* means, "empowered to prosper." People tend to use the word blessed casually. However, it is important to realize that when you are blessed you are truly empowered to prosper.

Luke 11:9

In this verse, Jesus is speaking: "And I say unto you, ask and it shall be given to you, seek and you shall find. Knock and it shall be opened unto you. For everyone that asks receives, he that seeks finds, to him that knocks it shall be opened." Jesus continues, "If a son shall ask bread of any of you that is a father, will he give him a stone? If he asks for a fish, will he instead of a fish, give him a serpent or if he shall ask an egg, will he offer him a scorpion?"

If your child asks you for bread, are you going to give him a stone, a rock? "Here, little Johnny with your little new teeth, chew on that!" Now Johnny is running around looking like he bit a brick! But even natural people, understanding natural things, would not do that to their child. Jesus was saying, "If you ask me for anything, I am not going to give you demonic things or devilish things in return for what you ask me for." He said, "I am God and I am good. So, therefore, if you understand naturally how to take care of your children, then how much more do I know how to take care of you? But if you don't ask, you have not because you ask not!"

So then He asks, "How much more shall your heavenly Father give the Holy Spirit to them that ask it?" Now, are you ready? "As He was casting out a devil, it was dumb, and it came to pass and when the devil was gone out, the dumb spake. And the people wondered and some of them said, 'He cast out devils through Beelzebub the chief of the devils, the lord of flies'; and others tempting him, sought a sign from heaven, but He knowing their thoughts, said, 'Every kingdom divided against itself is brought to desolation. A house divided against itself falls. If Satan also be divided against himself, how shall his kingdom stand?'"

Jesus just finished saying that if you ask for something from God, He gives you good things, never something demonic. Then He goes and casts out the dumb spirit from the child; notice the spirit was dumb, therefore, the child was dumb. This means that because the spirit couldn't speak, the child couldn't speak.

Physical attributes in some people are a manifestation of a spiritual attack in their lives. So when Jesus cast it out, they said, "He cast out devils by Beelzebub the Lord of flies! He's able to tell him to get out because He's of Satan himself!"

But Jesus has just said that what is good is good! What is evil is evil! Then He has clarified that every house divided against itself is not able to stand. He was not talking about the kingdom of God; He was referring to Satan's kingdom. So nothing good will come from Satan. That is why Satan only wants to steal, kill and destroy! Satan will not bring anything good into your life! So Jesus was rectifying and telling them, "Listen, if I am your Father, all you have to do is ask. Because I understand that no kingdom divided against itself shall stand, as God I will not use evil; and as Satan, the devil will not use good." They are contrary to each other; they are polar opposites.

Jesus was saying that if you ask anything of God — anything you ask of Him — if you ask, He will give it. If you knock, it will be opened. If you seek it, you will find it. Some people don't want to seek the truth; they're afraid they might actually find it! Some people might as well be saying, "I'd rather live in darkness and not know better."

Ephesians 6:10

This Scripture does not say, "Finally my brethren, be strong in the Lord and the power of your might." Nor, "Be strong in the Lord and the power of your neighbor's might." It doesn't even say, "Be strong in the Lord and in the power of your pastor's might."

God is telling you, "Be strong in God, and the power of God's ability. Put on the whole armor of God that you may be able to stand against the wiles of the devil." Do you remember the Road Runner cartoon and the character Wile E. Coyote? Why do you think he was called Wile E.? It's this word, *wiles*. The strategies, the plans. Wile E. must have had a credit card at Acme company because he bought everything he could find from Acme Co. Yet he still could never catch that roadrunner.

There are wiles and strategies that Satan habitually tries to use on you. You must understand that you have been blessed with all spiritual blessing; therefore, by no means will anything hurt you. Satan has a plan and a strategy to trick you. And if you don't *know* your authority and your ability, then he will trick you and get you to *think* that you *don't have* that authority and that ability by "tying you to a tree" when you're young. So as you're growing up, you don't know any better, and you fight against that "tree" until he breaks your spirit! Now, as an adult, you run around with a defeated mentality that believes, "This is my lot in life, this is just who I am and what I'm going to have to do."

You don't realize that you have been given all spiritual blessing and have been enabled and empowered through Christ to break every demonic stronghold in your life! But you must understand the difference between the power and the authority! Because sometimes in power, you won't feel like praising Him!

Sometimes by your power, you won't feel like giving Him all the glory. Sometimes in your power, you will feel like you can't win! But understand something: The Bible tells us that greater is He that is in us than he that is in the world! And He has overcome them because that's the truth, Ruth!

1 Peter 5:6

"Humble yourselves therefore under the mighty hand of God." Some people are so narcissistic and prideful that they cannot humble themselves. "Humble yourselves therefore under the mighty hand of God that He may exalt you in due time." He exalts you! Remember that Jesus gave his disciples a reminder to be humble in Luke 14:9-11 saying something like, "Don't you go into the wedding and go sit in the best seats. Just in case they decide to ask you to get up and go to the back, you should sit in the back and be humble and let them call you forward to a better seat!" He tells you that once you humble yourself before God, then cast all of your care upon Him for He cares for you. It is a measure of attitude and how we approach God.

Here's what people do. They say, "God, I command You to take care of my problems and here are my cares!" Where's the humility?

"God I know I can't do this, I need your help. I've got to give it to You because I can't do it." Humbly approach your Lord God, not commanding Him; God ain't your waiter.

"Cast your care upon Him." Humble yourself; give him your cares. He says, "Because, be sober be vigilant, your adversary the devil, as a roaring lion walks about seeking whom he may devour." Not *will* devour, nor does it say *can* devour. Why am I pointing that out? Because "may" implies permission! Doesn't it?

If you ask me, "Can I play this?" I don't know, can you? Are you able to or capable of playing it? But when you say, "May I play it," you're asking for permission. If Satan can only devour whom he may destroy, that now gives you the understanding that it is by your authorization that you will go through what you go through.

"Well, Satan's attacking me!" Really? Well, let's get into our authority for a moment and let's bind that, let's rebuke that, let's tell him to stop in the name of Jesus! A lion, when coming into its prey's ground or territory, will sometimes roar down because that roar will echo. The sound seems to come from every which direction. All the antelopes (and whatever else they eat) at that point don't know from whence it comes so everybody scatters, running in all directions. Understand this: If he roared straight at them they'd know, "Oh he's coming from that way! Everybody go that way!"

The Word says the devil roams around like a roaring lion seeking whom he may destroy. When he roars, the animals scatter. And the one that goes the wrong way ... well, you don't see a lion run into the middle of the herd. They wait for the one that's sickly, for the one that can't run as fast as the others, for the one that doesn't know its authority, for the one that is not with the crowd! And then they run after that one and devour that one!

But like those lions, Satan is looking for the one who gives permission and license for him to walk into his or her life and destroy it! "Seeking whom he may devour; Whom resist steadfast in the faith knowing that the same afflictions are accomplished in your brethren that are in the world, but the God of all grace who has called us to his eternal glory by Christ Jesus that after ye have suffered awhile make you perfect, established, strengthened, and settle you. To Him be the glory and dominion forever and ever" (1 Peter 5:9-11). Peter doesn't say go out there and beat that lion up, he doesn't say go out there and shoot the lion, he says you must resist, steadfast in the faith knowing that the God of all grace will perfect you and establish you.

People don't realize that what they're going through is part of the process of God establishing them! God is perfecting in them that which He wants from them! They think things like, "Well, I just don't want to deal with this anymore!"

But when you understand that you have been blessed with all spiritual blessing then you understand that you don't have *personal power*; you have *spiritual authority*. And God, who gave you spiritual power and authority, told you to resist in the faith. Why would he tell believers to resist in the faith if it was not possible? He wasn't talking to Himself; He was talking to you.

Peter said, resist in the faith. This means you have to understand that you are capable of resisting Satan in the faith. How do you do that? Paul said when you have done all to *stand, stand therefore*! You don't give one inch! Listen to me! I am literally at a place where Satan is not allowed to have a single thing that belongs to me! Not one penny, not one nickel, not anything! If it belongs to me, then, Satan, get your hands off!

And I am standing wherever I need to stand to believe God for whatever God has asked me to do. And let me tell you something, if you are not part of the plan of God, you will have little to no authority. Some people think they can speak to these

things and all this prosperity will fall into their laps devoid of purpose. It doesn't work that way. "I just want a Lamborghini! I just want this; God is going to bless me with that!" How does God's Kingdom benefit from you to driving around in a Lamborghini? If you are active in the things of God and you get blessed with an extravagantly expensive sports car, that is a whole different story! I vehemently believe that God wants to bless his people beyond all measure and am not suggesting that His people should not expect to have the best. But if someone is sitting at home doing absolutely nothing for the Kingdom, not helping anybody, and not serving in the body, that person needs to know that God's authority is delegated to those who will use it for His glory. That is, He wants His light to be seen in you!
Isaiah 1:19

We completely understand that we are unable to earn blessings. However it is the willing and obedient who will eat the good of the land. According to Isaiah 1:19, "If ye be willing and obedient, ye shall eat the good of the land."

Some people are on this side of the fence doing the will of God, serving God and they don't even know that a 100-dollar bill is sitting in the jewelry box. Problems come into their life and they think, "What do I do now?" Take your authority over it. It is simple: If you own a home, and I walk into your home and I say, "This home is now mine," you would probably tell me, "You'd better get on out of here." Right?

Yet Satan walks into people's lives, and they have authority over him, and here's the sad part: The day you get to see who Satan really is, you will see how puny and nothing he is and you are going to be shocked. You are going to say, "Oh my God, I ran from that? This is the one that was stirring up all this trouble?" Because the reality is this: In everything that belongs to you, if you are doing what God has asked you to do, then you have been blessed with all spiritual blessing and you walk in authority. And as you walk in that authority, in everything that comes against you, you have the authority to speak to it and it must respond, it must obey! And that is not because of how great you are; that is because of how great Jesus is. The reality of all of your power is vested in Jesus.

In Acts 19, the seven sons of Sceva tried to cast out devils. They had seen Paul do it, and so they figured they could do it. They mimicked what they saw and they went up to a demon-possessed man and said, "I cast you out by the Jesus whom Paul preached!" They had no real personal revelation of the name of Jesus. But because authority is delegated in Christ, mighty through God, when they went and spoke to the demons, do you know what the demons did? The demons stripped those seven sons of Sceva butt-naked and beat them, sent them running. The sons of Sceva did not understand that it was not power that cast out demons; it was delegated authority.

Some believers have been fighting Satan, not getting the victory, and have been wondering why they are so tired. Why would I fight with somebody that God already whooped? When David ran to the battle, he said to Goliath, "You come to me with a sword and a spear, but I come to you in the name of the Lord, for the battle is not mine, but it is God's!"

Like David, you need to understand that in some of the things you're going through, the battle is not yours; it is God's! And if you would get out of the way, you would not get shot so much! What you need to do is step back into your authority and say, "I come against that right now in the name of Jesus. Father, I thank You that my children will not be strung out. Father, I thank You that my children will be safe. Father, I thank You that I have authority in their lives and that I come against every sickness that comes against them. Father, I thank You right now that my body is healed and whole in the name of Jesus. Father I thank You that … (fill in the blank!)

"Satan, you get out of my marriage! You get out of my relationships! Satan, I don't care where you go, but you got to get up out of here!" Some people are afraid that Satan might hear them! But that is the point. He needs to hear you.

We must be like a child in some ways. Kids dare to have imagination and boldness. Kids will jump off the dresser thinking they are 10 feet tall and bulletproof. Somewhere along the line, they hit their head a few times and they become afraid of the floor. They become afraid of hitting stuff, and then they stop daring to dream. The tragic part is that spiritually we do the same thing. We try to stand in our authority, we try to rebuke something, it seems like it doesn't respond, and then we think, "Well it must not work."

The reality is that it has to work because God is not a man such as should lie. And it only works if you work it. Like soap, it will only make you clean if you use it. I have never seen a bar of soap jump off the countertop and wash somebody. You can't walk around with a bar of soap in your pocket and think that you are automatically clean. You must use it! I want you to have so much ammunition to understand your authority in Christ, because you must know this: You have been blessed with all spiritual blessing. You have to know that God has vested His power and strength in you by delegating authority, by giving you the ability to have dominion over these things.

Once you speak to Satan's scheme then don't let doubt set in. Once doubt sets in, it (whatever "it" is) is back. Why should it leave? Demons are like stray cats. If you are used to entertaining them, if you start hearing from them, they keep talking to you. Then they call all their buddies in, "Hey! Over at so-and-so's house! He listens to us, he likes us!" And they start coming to that bowl of milk and now, all of a sudden, demons will be following you, talking to you, revealing things to you, influencing you.

Although many think psychics are charlatans, I believe psychics are real. Those mediums that see people —"I see dead people" — they are real! They don't really see the dead people; they see familiar spirits. When you get people who are used to yielding to that sort of thing spiritually, then suddenly they can sense things spiritually, they are right. They are accurate to a point, but what they see is not of God, because it brings no glory to God.

If God reveals something to you, He will always reveal to you why He revealed it to you and what He wants you to do about it. If God revealed it then He is giving you authority to deal with it. That is why you can deal with everything that comes against your life by the power of the Word.

Now here's the problem: If you don't know the Word of God, then you can't speak the Word can you? That is why some Christians are in the middle of a spiritual gunfight with a little pocketknife. They cry, "Leave me alone!"

And demons respond, "Why should I leave you alone?"

"Because I said so! I'm tired of you! I'm sick and tired of being sick and tired!" But the moment you say, "The reason why I need you to step out of my body and leave my body alone is because by His stripes I am healed," they have to respond with something like, "Wait a minute, by His stripes ... whoa, that's in the Bible, let's go! Come on, oppression! Come on, cancer! We've got to go find somebody that doesn't know any better."

It is absolutely crucial that you understand your authority.

Chapter Two: Power or Authority

Power and authority are not always the same thing. In authority comes delegated power, but power and authority are not the same. The believer in Christ must understand that physically he or she may not have the power or the strength to do something, but having authority allows that believer to command it to be done and it will be done. Like the vested power of a police officer's badge, uniform, squad car, flashing lights and gun, this authority is not based on the believer's personal strength, but on the authority inherent in Christ's name.

Ephesians 6:12

According to Ephesians 6:12, "we wrestle not against flesh and blood but against principalities, against powers, against rulers of the darkness of this world, against spiritual wickedness in high places." To shed further light, I believe that there are a few questions that need to be clarified for more understanding. Is God in control of everything that happens on Earth? Is God sovereign? In other words, does He have supreme authority over everything on the Earth? Is He in control of everything on the Earth?

The Bible tells is that we don't wrestle against flesh and blood; in other words, we don't wrestle against people, we wrestle against the principalities and powers that operate through people. Paul says here that you don't wrestle against another person, but you wrestle against the demonic influence in or around that person.

If you own a house and the house has termites, do you have termites inside your body? The house has them; you are not the house, are you? But you live in the house. If your house has termites, eventually your house will have structural problems, because the termites will tear up your house. Your body can be compared to a house because you are a spirit and you live in a body and you possess a soul.

1 Thessalonians 5:23

"And the very God of peace sanctify you wholly; and I pray God your whole spirit and soul and body be preserved blameless unto the coming of our Lord Jesus Christ."

Some people are possessed; some people are not. Possession means that Satan has completely taken over a person's spirit, body and soul. Spitting pea soup, head spinning ... possession. However, can you live in a house that has termites without having termites yourself? If you are a spirit and you live in a body, your body can be oppressed; your soul can be oppressed.

Remember David talking to himself in Psalms, saying, "Why art thou cast down, oh my soul? Why art thou disquieted within me?" He said, "Hope in God! For He healeth thy infirmities." See, the infirmities and problems are always resident in the soul — the mind, will and emotions. So, if we are not the body, and we are not a soul, we are a spirit. Then, if we live in the house, the house can have termites can't it? The house can have demonic oppression can't it? Marcus Tullius Cicero once said, "Diseases of the soul are more dangerous and more numerous than those of the body." So your body and your soul can be demonically oppressed, yet your spirit is not.

The words, "We wrestle not against flesh and blood," help us to understand that the problems we face in life are not because of individuals; they're because of what is operating through that individual. So when you are dealing with people who are, for example, stubborn to the things of God, those people may say things like, "Well, I love God; I'm just ... you know, I've got things to do so I'm not coming to church."

If I call my wife and I say, "I love you, but I ain't coming home. ..." Come on, let's think about that for a minute! Demons know these things and they understand that if they can keep you out of the house of God, if they can keep you away from the anointing and the presence of God, if they can keep you separated from where your supply comes from, then they have a right to operate in your life undetected! We are not wrestling against flesh and blood; we are wrestling against principalities and powers! The world does not understand this. So they run around thinking, "I'm free! I'm doing whatever I want to do." A life without Christ is not free. It is bound to fear, to speculation, to feelings, to emotions; it is just plain bound. The Bible says, "Whom the Son sets free is free indeed!"

Ephesians 2:1-2

"And you hath He quickened, who were dead in trespasses and sins; Wherein in time past ye walked according to the course of this world, according to the prince of the power of the air, the spirit that now worketh in the children of disobedience."

If I put a mouse into a little maze, and that maze has only one direction to go, and I put a piece of cheese at the end, does that rodent choose its own path to get to that cheese? No, it follows what? My course, the course I laid out for it.

Likewise, Ephesians 2:1-2 is saying that when you were dead in your sins, when you were in the world, you walked according to a path that Satan had already laid out. That is, according to the prince of the power of the air, that spirit that now works in the children of disobedience, you were walking in a path that Satan had already planned for you. And these people who say, "I'm free to do whatever I want to do!" No, they are not. They are walking in a path that Satan has already prepared for them in order for them to be destroyed.

"Well, I'm free!" they cry. No, the Bible says, you're not; you're free when you believe in Christ! You are free when you have been saved! You are free when you are free to walk with God! But until that moment, until you have come to your conversion experience, you are not free! You are walking in a plan that Satan has already devised against you!

The word meaning "according to" in the Greek is KATA. A similar word, *kata*, is used in martial arts. It is a Japanese word describing detailed patterns of movements. When I was younger, I practiced martial arts. We were graded for belt promotion on our kata, our ability to execute a set series of predefined maneuvers. Many people in the world feel like they are free and believe themselves to be free, but, in fact, they are not. They walk according to the course of this world in a predefined pattern of movements that the world has already set up. Such people don't even see how they are conforming to Satan's pattern, so they live in bondage not realizing that they are wrestling with demons, principalities, and powers!

Ephesians 2 continues in verse 3, "We have had our conversation in times past in the lusts of our flesh fulfilling the desire of our flesh and of the mind and were by nature the children of wrath even as others. But God Who was rich in mercy, for His great law wherewith He loved us even when we were dead in sins has quickened us together with Christ, by grace are you saved, and He has raised us up together and made us sit together in heavenly places in Christ Jesus, that in the ages to come He might show the exceeding riches of His grace and kindness towards us in Christ Jesus!"

He quickened whom together? He quickened us, the believers in Christ! But God who was rich in mercy did not leave His people here without help! He put His people here with the grace and the riches and the inheritance of the saints and He put us up with Christ together!

As Christians, we must realize that we are fighting against spiritual things. We must be absolutely clear and sure to know our spiritual authority, because if we don't know who we are in Christ, defeat is assured. Simply being saved does not make Christians victorious; having a renewed mind and being skillful in the Word of God does. Plenty of Christians today are saved yet not victorious. They deal with the same oppression or depression that comes with life in the world.

From beginning to end, the book of Ephesians is six chapters, and it covers these three topics: how to *sit*, how to *walk* and how to *stand*. Sitting refers to your position. If I walk into Home Depot and I start giving their employees orders, do they follow my orders? Am I the boss there? This illustrates the idea of position. Before I start barking out orders, I must hold the position of boss. That is, I must be the boss positionally. If you understand that concept, then you understand that you have to know where you sit first before you start saying anything.

Next in Ephesians, Paul talks about how to walk, that is, how a Christian is supposed to live out his or her salvation. The idea of "walk" means, "this is how you live." You can't play with Satan all day and then expect to be able to tell him to go away from you! You may say, "Satan, I don't want to play with you anymore," but the problem is that once you have invited him in, he tries hard to stay in.

My grandmother used to say, "Houseguests are like fish; after three days they start to stink." Satan gets in there and hangs out. So Ephesians tells you how to walk out your life, how to live! People don't want to hear that. Here's what everybody wants to hear: "Just tell me I'm okay. Just tell me God loves me the way I am." God loves you despite the way you are. There's a difference, because He loves you too much to leave you in that state.

Then Paul talks about standing. What does standing mean? It means that you are standing against the attack that comes into your life, because how you respond to attack is how you live. A person who is under attack exhibits certain signals in his or her body language. That is why Paul said, "I long to see your face that I may perfect what is lacking in your faith."

In 1 Thessalonians 3:10, Paul wrote, "Night and day praying exceedingly that we might see your face, and might perfect that which is lacking in your faith."

When you are under attack, your face always will reveal what is lacking in your faith. So the Christian's challenge is to understand that "sit, walk, stand" means, "this is where you sit positionally; this is where you walk; this is how you live; and then stand — this is how you stand against the attack of the enemy on your life. If you think that everything you go through is flesh, you are going to want to punch everyone in the mouth. And the problem is you can swing until you pass out, but if you don't understand authority you will have movement but zero momentum. Rocking back and forth in a rocking chair is movement, but you are not going anywhere.

This is why the world struggles with young people. We adults have allowed them to disregard our authority and respect only our power. But when power is no longer enough — when the spanking doesn't do anything — they have no respect for authority, because see authority says, "Do this."

"Why?" they say.

"Because I said so."

"Well, I need a better explanation."

"No you don't!" Nowadays the popular childrearing philosophy says, "You have to explain it to them and make sure they understand and then give them a cognitive understanding of what you're desiring. ..." Listen! I'm going to spank that "beauteous" maximus until this kid's cerebral cortex gets a new revelation! I don't have to explain myself to him!

"Okay, Johnny listen," says the parent, "this is why we have to do this." Johnny is three years old! But here is what happens: we get our kids to respect power. If we can physically corral them and get them to do what we want them to do, no longer is authority the issue. So when they are out of the parent's sight, parental authority has no value, and the parent is always wondering where the kid is and what he or she is doing.

I don't know what happened with me, but I just assumed my mama knew everything. I assumed that she knew whether I was in her sight or out of her sight, what was going on. I assumed she knew because somehow she did know. Nowadays, media has a huge influence. We grownups watch this stupid stuff and we let our kids watch it, and in these shows the kids are always smarter than the parents. I watched a documentary on *The Cosby Show* and one of the principles that it was founded on was the idea that at the end of the show, the parents always were smarter than the kids. But these days, TV depicts dad as a bumbling idiot. He can't do anything right, degrading and denigrating the male role model in the home! So men grow up who don't know their responsibilities because no one has stepped up and said, "This is your position of authority."

Matthew 28:18-20

Then Jesus came to them and said, "All authority in heaven and on earth has been given to me. Therefore go and make disciples of all nations, baptizing them in the name of the Father and of the Son and of the Holy Spirit, and teaching them to obey everything I have commanded you. And surely I am with you always, to the very end of the age" (NIV).

At this point in Matthew 28, Jesus has now been resurrected. Most Christians understand the gospel in terms of Jesus going to the cross. But let's go a little bit deeper with our gospel and turn it from a *cross* gospel to a *throne* gospel. By that I mean this: Jesus dying on the cross. Most people see a crucifix and often see a representation of Christ on it. I wear a cross around my neck, but there is no Jesus on it. Jesus is not on the cross anymore.

The cross is a symbol of our Savior's death, which is beautiful to a certain degree in terms of our redemption. But just to be redeemed and not be equipped is a problem. For me to give you a job and not give you the equipment to accomplish the job is one-sided. You need to understand that on the other side of that cross are a resurrection and the ascension to the throne! This is where it no longer represents only Christ's death but also His overcoming the grave, death and Satan, thereby equipping us to do the same.

When Jesus said that all power has been given to Him, He had just been resurrected and He was telling His closest followers, "Listen to Me! All power has been given to Me. So now I need you all to go! Not for vacationing purposes, but to go and to teach them that don't know! Make disciples out of them! Teach them what they need to know to walk in the power and the authority in which I walk again! Because I now have it!" Why does He now have it? Because he descended; Ephesians 4:9 says, "Now that He ascended, what is it but that He first descended?" So what did He do?

The book of Genesis says that man was given dominion. Man had dominion until Eve was deceived and she led Adam astray. Because of the fall of man, authority was taken and dominion was taken from man due to Satan's deception. Then

33

authority passed to Satan. So when Ephesians 6:12 says, "… the god of this world, against principalities and power," then this is what we wrestle against. Who are we wrestling against? Satan, the god of this world. Jesus said, "All power has been given unto Me," so if Satan had known what he was really doing, he would have never crucified Christ! So because of Satan's arrogance and stupidity, Jesus descended and then overcame and ascended.

Why would Jesus say, "All power has been given unto me, now go"? If I told you, "I now own all of the world! Now go!"

"Go do what?" you might ask. Anything you want to do. I own it now! And if we have a relationship, and if I own it, then you have access to it, don't you?

I have heard it said, "My wife's money is her money; and my money is our money." So if I win a million dollars, my wife also wins because I'm in relationship and fellowship with her. Jesus said, "All authority has been given unto Me, now go. Go teach everybody what I taught you. Go show everybody what I showed you. That's a command; that's not an option."

He didn't say, "Just come to church and sit in a chair." He said, "Now go and teach everything that I have taught you. Make disciples and expand the Kingdom. This is the Great Commission." Sometimes people do not realize that Jesus is talking here to each and every person in the body of Christ.

Luke 10:17-19

In this passage from Luke's gospel, the seventy-two whom Jesus had appointed and sent throughout Israel returned with joy and said, "Lord, even the demons submit to us in your name." He replied, "I saw Satan fall like lightning from heaven. I have given you authority to trample on snakes and scorpions and to overcome all the power of the enemy; nothing will harm you" (NIV).

The disciples are all excited that the demons are subject to them through the name of Jesus. But Jesus responds with the fact that He witnessed Satan fall from heaven. This may seem to be a curious response. We know that Satan fell from heaven a long time before Jesus was ever born on earth of Mary, which means that Jesus always existed. So the Person you know as Jesus the man from Nazareth is only one phase of His ministry.

But Jesus said, "I saw Satan fall! That's why the demons are subject to you." In other words, "Satan does not have power over anything concerning Me because I always was there in the beginning, even when Eve messed up!"

The Bible says Jesus is from everlasting to everlasting! He always was and will always be! Jesus had three phases to his ministry. Prior to being born as a human baby of Mary, He had His pre-incarnated ministry. That was followed by His earthly ministry and finally His post-resurrection priestly ministry. In essence, Jesus was explaining to the disciples that He understands that Satan has been defeated and has no ability to stand against God. The last time He tried to directly stand against God, he ended up on the floor. Falling like a lightning bolt — now that's fast!

Then Jesus continues, "Behold, I give unto you power to tread on serpents and scorpions and over all the power of the enemy." Nothing shall hurt you because you have power over all the enemy's tricks, plans, pursuits, and attacks. You have to be clear that you have authority over them all, in Jesus' name. This pronouncement does not mean that we should dance and party with snakes. If you see stuff like that, avoid it at all cost. If you see people start dancing around with snakes, it is time to go. This is an instance of people taking the Bible and twisting it into a place it should not go.

Jesus says, "Not withstanding in this. ..." In other words, "Although I've given you power, don't be rejoicing that spirits are subject to you, but rather rejoice because your name is written in heaven." To Jesus, it wasn't about the power because He understood authority and power; He wasn't thinking about these terms like his disciples were. They were used to getting their tails whooped constantly by the devil.

We have all heard people say things like, "Don't say it too loud, the devil might hear you!" Really? We have to have the confidence like Jesus does and let Satan know that we are going to step on Satan's neck every chance we get!

Always remember to not get power hungry, but rejoice that your name is written in heaven. Rejoice that you are saved! But remember that the authority is in the name of Jesus, not in you yourself. If you ever try to rebuke Satan without the power of God through the authority that only Jesus Christ brings ... well, it was nice knowing you.

Unfortunately, we live in a narcissistic society. I was sitting in a counseling meeting with someone at my executive international headquarters, Starbucks. I heard somebody at the next table saying something about this woman who was sick and that the "name it and claim it bunch" would say she doesn't have faith. Man, I wanted so badly to get up and go tell that person, "What are you talking about? First of all, we please God by faith."

Don't act like faith is a bad thing, because faith is not a bad thing and if she doesn't have faith, then what are you doing to help build her faith so she could get healed? The Bible says that we shall lay hands on the sick and they shall recover! If she doesn't have the faith, then get up and go lay hands on her! Don't sit here and talk about what everybody else isn't doing! We don't have a name-it-and-claim-it theology. If God said we can have it, then it's been revealed in the Bible. There are 7,000 promises written in this Bible that concern me. If one of those 7,000 is something that I need, I am now not "naming and claiming" something — I am now coming into agreement with my Daddy's plan for my life! And I am commanding *it*, not Him! It's not "name it and claim it"; you can't arbitrarily come up with something and expect God to bless it! I abhor that stupidity! What kind of good news is it if you are not going to be blessed? What is the good news? That you're going to die? What is the good news? That you're going to be sick all your life? Who thinks that's good news?

Ephesians 1:18-23

Paul continues in Ephesians 1:18-23, saying, "The eyes of your understanding being enlightened; that ye may know what is the hope of His calling, and what the riches of the glory of His inheritance in the saints, and what is the exceeding greatness of His power to us-ward who believe, according to the working of His mighty power, which He wrought in Christ, when He raised Him from the dead, and set Him at His own right hand in the heavenly places, far above all principality, and power, and might, and dominion, and every name that is named, not only in this world, but also in that which is to come: and hath put all things under His feet, and gave Him to be the head over all things to the church, which is His body, the fulness of him that filleth all in all" (KJV).

Where is Jesus? In heavenly places. Jesus upon His resurrection has become the head of the body. We have become the body. Hence the term "the Body of Christ."

Years ago there was a TV show on which one of the recurring skits was called "The Head Detective." The Detective was a head with no body. And the criminals would try to run away and he would say, "Throw me at 'em!"

The floor is under my feet. I have a head, and I have a body. The Bible says that Jesus ascended to the right hand of God (and the right hand always reveals the power of God), and He has been raised up and is now the head of the body. Christians are to understand that we are the body, He is the head, and we sit together with Him, far above principality and power. If it is under His feet and you are the body, then positionally speaking, where is Satan in terms of Jesus? Under our feet! Then why are we wrestling with someone who is under our feet? The Bible says, "What is the exceeding greatness of the power to us who believe." That "us" is us! The reference to putting all things under His feet also means under his body (us) as well.

In Jesus' time, Jewish synagogues kept a teacher's chair on the platform. It was a seat of authority. According to *John Gill's Exposition of the Bible* and Vincent's *Word Studies in the New Testament*, it was the customary position of whoever read the Scriptures on Sabbath to be seated and teach. Some theologians have stated that an empty chair sat on the platform, and that chair was the chair of the coming Messiah. That chair remains empty because the Jewish people are waiting for the coming Messiah to take his seated position as the Messiah and Savior of the world. They are still waiting for the Messiah to show up. And when the

Messiah shows up, He will take His seat in that chair. This is significant when we read Luke chapter 4. We have to understand that Jesus was reading out of the Bible and He said, "The Spirit of the Lord God is upon me for He has anointed me to preach good tidings unto the meek," and He went through and started talking about who He was. The Bible says He closed the book and He sat down. All eyes were fixed upon Him and they were about to stone Him. Why? Because He read something? No. Because what He did was He sat down in that chair! And when he did that, the people were appalled. "No! The Messiah has not come yet! Nobody sits in that chair but the Messiah!"

Whether or not He sat in the Messiah's chair or in His position of authority to teach, we are not sure, but allegorically it still conveys the same message. By His action He was saying, "That throne is Mine! And I am going to sit in it because it belongs to Me." And so if He, as the head, is seated on the throne in heavenly places, and Satan is under His feet, then Satan is also under your feet! And that means you have authority over Satan! We are, in fact, positionally far above all principality, all power, all might, all dominion. Far above is where we sit. So now, here is the question: If you sit so far above, why are you trying to duke it out with Satan? Did He put some things under His feet or all things? Did He put a few things under His feet or all things? Obviously, the Bible says all!

Colossians 2:13-15

"And you, being dead in your sins and the uncircumcision of your flesh, hath he quickened together with Him, having forgiven you all trespasses; blotting out the handwriting of ordinances that was against us, which was contrary to us, and took it out of the way, nailing it to His cross; and having spoiled principalities and powers, he made a show of them openly, triumphing over them in it" (KJV).

We were quickened together with Him! At the moment Jesus ascended to His throne at the right hand of God, we were quickened or made alive with Him to be seated in the same heavenly places. "Blotting out the handwriting of the ordinances that were against you" means blocking out the punishment of the law, "which was contrary to us, He took it out of the way and nailed it to the cross." Sickness — He nailed it to the cross. Oppression — He nailed it to the cross. Depression — nailed to the cross. Poverty was nailed to the cross!

The Bible says, "And having spoiled principalities and powers, He made a show of them openly, triumphing over them in it." Glory to God! That means He overcame the grave, and He did it publicly! He did not do it in hiding; He did it publicly! When they killed Jesus on the cross, He overcame all these things! Three days later, He arose and He came up out of the grave and He made a show of them openly! Satan messed up. Because they killed an innocent man, Jesus was able to take the authority from Satan because he broke the rules! The Word says here that He made a show of them openly. Just as in the garden Satan was able to take the authority from Adam and Eve because they broke the rules, in a similar fashion, Jesus was able to take back the authority because Satan broke the rules.

Back in those days, when an army defeated another army, the conquerors would bring the conquered in chains along with the spoils on display before the king. They would parade them in front of the king so that the king could see the conquered soldiers and people who had been made part of his kingdom. Jesus made a show of Satan openly to make it clear that not only is God truly the authority but also that Satan and his devils have now been conquered.

Christians need to know that we are dealing with someone who has already been defeated. For example, imagine that you are the parent of a child who misbehaves. As a responsible parent, you smack him on his little behind or maybe place him in time out. The child is now punished! He has now been corrected! Now imagine that you turn your back and walk away and this child sticks out his tongue at you. You may not have seen him do that, but he still can, can't he?

Here is my point: Although our enemy has been defeated, he finds every chance he can to mess with you. And if you don't realize that he has already been whooped and that you have authority over him, he will do whatever he can to mess with you. If you don't know your authority, he will take advantage of your ignorance. So now he is out there sticking out his tongue at you, he is messing you with, he is getting into your family, he is attacking your life, he is attacking your thinking. Feeling helpless, you ask God to help you defeat the enemy, when the reality is He already has.

If you listed your house for sale, and I bought it from you, we would sign papers giving me the deed to the house, and you would give me the keys to your house, which is now my house. Let's say that the next day I drive to work, and on my way home I call you and say, "Hey, could you let me in?" What would you say?

Jesus said, "I have given you all power!" We are asking God to help us, but He has already given us the keys to His

Kingdom! He has invested authority in you! So what are you supposed to do? Say, "Satan, in the name of Jesus, get your hands off of my finances! In the name of Jesus, get your hands off my children! I bind you right now in the name of Jesus! Don't you ever step foot in my house again!"

Not, "God, if it be your will, please help me..." I am not making light of this situation or poking fun at people who struggle in this area, because I am trying to be honest. I want to help Christians see this truth. If somebody has given me the keys to a house I have purchased, why would I call the previous owner and say, "Hey, could you let me into the house?"

What did Jesus say? "It is finished!" Jesus did what He was supposed to do; now it is up to you to go (with the rest of the church) into all the world and preach the gospel and teach them what He taught you so that together we will have victory! People in the world are struggling and do not understand, and Satan has blinded them. I will never forget my authority! Why? Because Jesus invested it in me when He said, "Behold, I give you power."

Colossians 2:15 says, "Spoil them." Other translations say, "Put them to naught or paralyze." Some people will ask God to take away an addiction. Meanwhile the reality is that you will get attacked because Jesus did not take the principalities and powers out of the world. He paralyzed them and took their power from them. Imagine I put you in a room with a bunch of little kids and I come to you and say, "I took all their water guns, so none of them can squirt you." Are they still in the room with you? Will they still try to do stuff to you? But they cannot shoot you because I have stripped them.

That is what the Word is saying — He took away their ability to hurt you, but they are still going to be here for a while. 2 Thessalonians 2:6 says, "There is one who holdeth back and until he is removed from the earth, they are being held back." So there will come a time of what we know as "the tribulation," when the church is caught up out of this world and the hand that is holding back, the Holy Spirit, will release Satan to do whatever he wants to do. If you think it is bad now, wait until Christians are pulled up out of here! This is why you need to go and tell everybody you know, "Listen, get your relationship right with Jesus! Because when that trumpet sounds, it's too late!" When we are called up out of here, there is going to be a release of all evil like you have never seen before! And the One who is holding him back will walk away and let him go! And the people you love will be stuck being attacked because you would not say anything to them, because you wouldn't tell them.

People think the world is bad now. Wait until God takes the handcuffs off and says, "All right, I gave them all time to get it together. Satan, go on ahead." And for seven years, he will do whatever he wants to do. Then the Bible says that in the sky Jesus shall appear with us at his side to come back to the thousand-year rule to take back what belongs to Him with us. Then, the Bible says, at that time, the full light of God will be seen on this planet.

Can you imagine the throne of God descending onto this planet to where the fullness of who God is will be seen and all evil will be held at bay? Completely! Yes, the evil minions will be held at bay until their demise, that is, the lake of fire. You must understand that the only reason why you have authority and power is to go and tell everybody the good news.

Romans 5:17

Paul tells us here in Romans, "For if because of one man's trespass (lapse, offense) death reigned through that one, much more surely will those who receive [God's] overflowing grace (unmerited favor) and the free gift of righteousness [putting them into right standing with Himself] reign as kings in life through the one Man Jesus Christ (the Messiah, the Anointed One)" (AMP).

If Christ is the King of kings and the Lord of lords, and you are in Him, that makes you a king! It makes you a lord! But you need to understand that it is your authority that you must walk in! Do not sit there and act like God has to do it all! You are a king; you are a queen! You have authority! How will you reign as a king? Let me tell you what a king does: When a king decrees something, he doesn't ask for stuff. Kings do not ask for stuff. A king says, "This is law!" And when the king decrees it, that is the end of it and that settles it. The problem is, you are a spiritual king, yet you are asking Satan, "Would you please leave me alone?" And Satan's answer is, "No. Anything else?"

I used to train realtors to handle objections when they would do their listing appointments. I taught them that if a customer was to ask, "Can we negotiate your commission," my answer was, "No, anything else?" Simple, effective, and to the point. Why? Because my commission was not an option!

Likewise, Satan is not going to say, "Yeah, I'll leave you alone for a little while." His answer will be, "No!"

"Would you back off?"

"No."

"Would you get this addiction off of me?"

"No."

So what do I now have to do? I now have to command him! "So let me phrase this in a way that I don't have any dangling participles on my statements. Let me go! Get your hands off my children in the name of Jesus! I bind you! Get out of my life! Not simply now, but right now!"

So here is what happens: Remember when Jesus saw his disciples trying to cast the devil out of the little boy? Jesus walked up and they said, "Master, we've been trying."

And Jesus said, "Some demons can be dealt with only by prayer and fasting." He said, "Now you get out of him, you come out right now." And the King James Bible says the boy fell to the ground and was "rent sore." In other words, the demon tore him up and then left. Afterward, the torn-up boy fell as dead, and everybody around said, "That boy is dead! You didn't cast any devil out of him. You killed him!"

My point is that sometimes we think when we have cast them out or we have told Satan to leave us alone, we think all of a sudden he backs off and that's it. But let me tell you something, Jesus commanded him to leave and that demon said, "I'm taking the opportunity to get one more attack in! I'm leaving, but I'm kicking everything out the door when I go!"

You have to understand that that sort of thing happens, because sometimes you may have spoken to demonic situations, and the demon didn't respond immediately. And when he kicked the door in again, you may have said, "Oh that didn't work." And the moment you question your authority that way, the demonic forces take your doubt as an opportunity to not leave. Christian, you have got to know that when you speak to something in the name of Jesus and in agreement with God's Word, it has to happen. God tells us, "My Word shall not return void that it shall go and accomplish the thing which I sent it to!" God's Word can never fail! If you have failed, it was you, not his Word! If anything has failed, the thing itself has failed; it cannot be blamed on His Word! Because God said His Word will never return void.

Then Jesus said, "I have given you the keys to the kingdom. What you bind on earth shall be bound in heaven. What you loose on earth shall be loosed in heaven." In other words, what you permit will stay. I know people who are harassed in their mind. Spirits are always working havoc in their thought life. They can't ever seem to understand why they go from depression to problems. They feel insecure, they feel hurt, they feel hateful, they feel anger, they feel rage. And they go through all these emotions all at the same time, and they wonder, "Am I crazy?"

"No!" I say. You are being harassed! Now what do you do about that harassment? Either you get into a place where someone has an anointing that can break that yoke, or you get yourself together, get your relationship right with God and then you say, "Devil! In the name of Jesus, I will not yield to that! I break the power of that addiction right now in the name of Jesus!" And it goes. It goes because of Jesus, not you. You do not have to be perfect, you do not have to be the best; all you have to do is know Jesus.

Acts 19:11-20

Luke reports in the book of Acts, "And God wrought special miracles by the hands of Paul: So that from his body were brought unto the sick handkerchiefs or aprons, and the diseases departed from them, and the evil spirits went out of them. Then certain of the vagabond Jews, exorcists, took upon them to call over them which had evil spirits the name of the Lord Jesus, saying, 'We adjure you by Jesus whom Paul preacheth.' And there were seven sons of one Sceva, a Jew, and chief of the priests, which did so. And the evil spirit answered and said, 'Jesus I know, and Paul I know; but who are ye?' And the man in whom the evil spirit was leaped on them, and overcame them, and prevailed against them, so that they fled out of that house naked and wounded. And this was known to all the Jews and Greeks also dwelling at Ephesus; and fear fell on them all, and the name of the Lord Jesus was magnified. And many that believed came, and confessed, and shewed their deeds. Many of them also which used curious arts brought their books together, and burned them before all men: and they counted the price of them, and found it fifty thousand pieces of silver. So mightily grew the word of God and prevailed."

The Sons of Sceva were professional exorcists. They saw Paul performing miracles and demonstrations of the spirit. Unfortunately for them, they figured it was easy to do. So they went, and they saw the people hounded by devils and they went to them and said, "Hey, in the name of Jesus whom Paul serves. ..." It became very obvious that they had no relationship with Christ, and the demons responded with "Jesus I know, Paul I know, but who are you?" They then responded with an all-out-embarrassing attack.

Why did they get sent running? Because they did not know that it was not about the Jesus *whom Paul served*. Christians cannot cast out anything or deal with anything demonic by the

Jesus that someone else serves. Christians must function by the Jesus that each one serves personally! The Jesus that the Christian knows by personal experience! And based on that authority that Jesus has put into the believer's life, then the believer speaks to it, not because of anybody else but through his or her own relationship with Christ that gives each believer authority!

For far too long, Christians have been mimicking and imitating spiritual warfare without realizing that a personal relationship and understanding are the keys to their authority in Christ. Although Polly the parrot may want a cracker, please be aware that Polly really doesn't know what a cracker is. Polly knows that when he imitates a sound pattern, then Polly receives a reward of some sort. Understanding, not imitation will bring true results.

You have been quickened together with Christ; you are not defeated. In a conversation with my spiritual father, he explained something to me. He said, "You know how many people have lost their faith because, for example, somebody died? And they're like, 'God, how come you didn't heal them? God, how come you didn't do this?' Here's the reality: What if God made the decision, 'I don't want them to suffer anymore'"?

See, the ultimate healing is death! Once you have passed into eternal life, all sickness shall pass away! Then neither shall there be any hurt, neither shall there be any tears! He shall wipe away all the tears from their eyes. There is no pain in heaven! What if He said, "I'm done watching them suffer." But let's flip to the other side: What if they never knew they had authority and didn't have to die? We don't blame them; it is not they are bad people, but what if no one ever taught them?

Jesus said, "Go ye and teach them what I taught you!" If nobody is going to teach them correctly, then here they are struggling, not knowing they could have had the power and the authority to deal with this stuff! And then their death becomes something Satan uses. "See, they died."

Here is an example: Imagine a doctor says, "You have cancer." Then suddenly, Satan says, "You know, your sister had cancer and she didn't make it. You know, your uncle had cancer, and he didn't make it." Now you are sitting there thinking, "Oh, my God!"

In these situations and times, you must remind yourself what The Bible says, that you shall live and shall not die. Christians have got to understand that in a time of attack against our faith, we must understand our position in Christ and be certain not to allow the condition of our circumstances to rule our lives. If you don't understand your position, victory is most assuredly lost. We as believers must be careful not to allow our circumstances and experiences to shape and mold our faith away from what the Word of God says.

In ancient times, when an individual wanted to approach a king, the king must acknowledge that person and lift his scepter to signal them to approach. Otherwise, people who had not been officially summoned were not allowed to approach and speak to a king.

It follows then that if you are seated in heavenly places at the right hand of the throne, then that means that anything that comes to talk to you must be acknowledged first! And if Satan is speaking in your ear and you have not acknowledged him, he is out of order! But do you know your authority to say, "You know what,

Satan? I'm not hearing that. Talk to the hand"? Because my God says I shall live and not die.

These are issues regarding authority that people struggle with in ignorance of the truth. I've watched people whose children are struggling with sickness over and over and over again, and sometimes I want to ask them if they understand their authority. You do not have to ask; all you have to do is say! Remember the woman who came to Jesus' feet in Mark 7:27, and she said, "I need healing for my daughter." And Jesus said, "It is not meet for me to cast the children's bread to a dog." He called her a dog! She responded, "Master, even the dog gets a crumb from the Master's table." It got his attention to such a point that he told her that she had great faith.

Now why did she come to Jesus for her child? Because she was the one who had authority over her child! She, because of her relationship and authority over the child, had authority over anything that came against her and her child! All she had to do was seek Jesus, and when He told her that her child was made whole, the Bible says from that hour her child was healed. Speak over your children and take authority over the things that are attacking them. Stand in your authority and say, "Hey! Hold up, devil! As for me and my house, we are going to serve the Lord! I bind you right now!"

There are times when I've had to go to my wife and say, "I don't need you to pray with me, I need you to pray for me. I don't have it in me, so I need you to pray for me." Why? Because we have authority in each other's lives because of our relationship. Husbands, do you have problems with your wife? Get on your knees! Wives, have you got problems with your husband? Get on your knees! Because there is something about you stepping into your authority and getting Satan out of your marriage, out of your life, out of your house, out of your family! It is time for the church to step up and take its authority and do what it was called to do! Walk in the greatness that you are called to be! You are not called to be wimps! You are called to be Christians! A Christian is a little Christ! You take your authority; you walk in what God has for you. Don't you accept anything less! Not a thing!

There are times when I'm thinking and praying, "God, I know you've got more for me." And God will say, "If you know that, then ask Me for it."

I'll say, "God, I ask you for the provision in my life."

Then He says, "Now, command Satan to let it go."

"Satan, I rebuke you and bind you in the name of Jesus. Let go of my provision."

Then God says, "Now, command your angels that do excel in strength to go get it." Understand this: In the book of Luke, Satan said that he will give this world and power to whom he wills. People think, "Well I'm just going to command Satan to give it to me."

No. It's not his will to give it to you, but he does have to let it go. Get the difference? Some people think, "Well, you know, God, if it be Thy will, if it be this way ... maybe some kind of ... how... sorta, woulda, shoulda. ..." And their language lacks authority and certainty. No, we must command Satan to take his hands off. "Take your hands off my child right now in the name of Jesus. You can go anywhere else you want to go, but you have got to leave here." When Satan asks why, your answer is a resounding, "Because in Jesus' name, that's why!"

At certain times Satan will remind you of your past mistakes and tell you that you are no good; you make mistakes! Let him know that you don't come before him in your authority. You are there by Jesus' authority.

Chapter Three: Releasing Authority

Moving beyond understanding our position in Christ and the authority that God has given us, we are going to take a slightly different direction. Many times in our lives, we put ourselves in positions where we have asked God to do things, we have prayed and said, "God help us, God do this, or God remove this temptation out of my life, or God remove Satan from me, etc." How many of us have done that? And then how many of us have become upset when the requested result never happened?

I understand what it feels like to struggle and to say, "God I need this removed." And no answer comes. I've known what it is like to say, "God take this thing away," and no answer comes.

At that point, most Christians begin to wonder, "What am I doing wrong? What am I saying wrong? Do I need to be more articulate in my prayers? Do I need to have the ability to eloquently communicate my prayers to the Most Holy and

Auspicious One in a way that will be a higher level of jargon and understanding? Maybe God only hears it in a certain way. ..." The reality is, that is not true, because He wants fellowship with you.

The Bible tells us that He knows what you need before you even ask for it. Therefore, the question becomes, why is it that it seems as if sometimes there are moments in our lives where we need God and it appears as though He does not respond. I am going to help you understand and get an answer so that you will never have to ask that question ever again.

Ephesians 6:12

This verse tells us, "For we wrestle not against flesh and blood, but against principalities, against powers, against rulers of the darkness of this world, against spiritual wickedness in high places." In other words, we do not wrestle against people; we wrestle against principalities and powers and against rulers of the darkness of this world. So we need to understand that this world has a system and the system of this world works a certain way.

Here is an example. In light of recent events, most people are well aware of the problems with our banking system. The better one's credit is in the banking system, the lower his or her interest rates are, which results in lower payments for that person. The person with poor credit is a higher risk to the bank, so that person gets a higher interest rate ... and higher payments. It's not that the banks won't lend their money to a person with poor credit, but they will charge that person extra to borrow the money. Then because that poor-credit/high-risk person struggles even more to pay more, and goes further into debt, which marks that person as an even higher credit risk.

Having been in banking a number of years, I understand this process. Although they may not have known the foreclosure market was going to happen the way it did, many of the key players in the financial markets in America knew it was coming. And they played and hedged their bets against it, knowing it was going to happen. These financial players make money when the market is either down or up.

The world's system is not designed to be ethical or moral. That is why it is so bizarre to me to hear people constantly saying, "Well this president should do that; this person should do that; this CEO should do that," and so on. When in the world, in the history of man, has government been the source of morality? When did we shift our authority over to their authority and expect our government to be the keepers of morality, instead of us being moral?

People do not realize that Satan is behind this system. He has created a way of conduct, a methodology, a program. And the beautiful thing is that God said, "I have translated you out of the kingdom of darkness into the light!" He has pulled you out of darkness not just so you could say, "I'm a Christian," but so that you could go back into that darkness and bring light to it!

But we — the church — have not realized that we don't wrestle against flesh and blood. Here is what happens: Something occurs in a Christian's life and it comes through a particular person; now this Christian person wants to bop the other person in the nose. Why? Because this Christian person is looking at the flesh and failing to realize that there are some attacks in his or her life that did not originate with flesh and blood. They originated because Satan himself has dispatched demonic forces to attack believers in Christ. Paul penned in 2 Corinthians 12 that he besought the Lord three times to get rid of a messenger of Satan, to take away from him this problem that he was dealing with. And God did not respond by informing Paul that he had authority over it; God told him, "My grace is sufficient." What He made clear for us is that we may go through situations, but the reality is that His grace will bring you through those times, that when the end comes, you shall inherit salvation.

You must endeavor to understand how to realize that there are certain situations you will go through in which you do not have the authority to say "stop it!" Because in the situation is something that God is about to do in your life. Oftentimes these situations exist to use the Christian to show forth God's glory!

Yet we become fixated on the problems and wonder why we have to deal with them. God, take this away from me! Often we do not realize that sometimes the answer is no. We think every answer should always be yes. "God, I want a million dollars!"

Sometimes the answer is, not now. And God has good reasons for that, such as, if He gave you a million dollars, you would lose your mind. Did you know that many people who win the lottery file bankruptcy within 5 years? Do you want to know why? Because when God brought the children of Israel out of Egypt, it took 40 years to get Egypt out of them. God did not bring them immediately into their Promised Land; He took them out of bondage first! He left them in the place of just enough.

The Lord's Prayer says, "Give us this day our daily bread." Do you know what that means? That is not your promised land. It means, "Keep me going for today." That is just enough. In the wilderness, they could not carry the bread anywhere. They could not go anywhere with it. They had to eat what they could eat and keep moving.

Although all promises in God are "yes and amen," we have to have the inward leading of the Holy Spirit in order to help us determine times and seasons. God had to use the wilderness situation to get Egypt out of the children of Israel, so that when they went into the Promised Land, when they walked into their blessing, they would not act like Egyptians. Because you cannot be an Egyptian and function correctly in a blessing place of God! You have got to know what the difference is! Otherwise, you will be walking into the Promised Land without even knowing that it is yours.

Before you enter your promised land, your thinking has to change. People struggle because they refuse to change the way they think. They are used to doing life a certain way. The Bible tells us to renew our minds. Prior to knowing Jesus, everything that I did burned up. I am aware of that. I have spent all my life doing different things that I thought were great, but prior to Jesus directing my path, all those things burned up. There is no record of it! It means nothing!

People wonder, "Pastor, why are you so adamant and pushing towards the things of God? Why are you so focused on the things of God? Why are you so fanatical about God?"

Here is why: I have got years that I want to make up for in which nothing I did was worth anything until I came to the knowledge of God in Christ. I now walk in the plan of God, realizing that all these things that I do for Him, I will see when I'm in heaven. Those things will not burn up when I stand before God and He says, "Well done!" That's all I want to hear! I understand that when I put myself in that state, and I'm mindful that nothing I did ever made any difference until I realized God's plan for me.

Mark Twain said, "The two most important days in your life are the day you are born and the day you find out why." God has a purpose for us. When I submit to His plan, then I get to see the lame walk, the blind see, and the deaf hear.

As submitted believers in Christ, we get to walk in the provision of God. We get to walk in the miracles of God because we know that God has a plan. This is where young people need to be paying attention! The world tries to get young people to think that their future is hopeless, when the reality is, without Christ it is hopeless. But the truth of the matter is once you have known and are in a faith-based relationship, not religion, but a relationship with Christ, your future is bright! Tomorrow will always be better than today! Always!

Sometimes we put ourselves in positions where we struggle and say, "Lord, help me. Help me Lord. Take this from me; I don't want to struggle anymore." But the reality is that as we understand these things in their proper context, we realize we have been taken out of this world's kingdom, yet we still live in this kingdom. We are in the world, but we are not of the world. If you got saved and then died, you would not have to put up with anything. That is how it would be if God just said, "All right, once they get saved, I'm bringing them home!" But He left you here for a purpose, to be in this world but not of it! So while we are in this world, we wrestle against principalities and powers. We wrestle against demonic influence and satanic attack. We have to learn how not to be afraid, and gain understanding — because we cannot fight without knowing how.

Romans 5:14

In his letter to the church at Rome, Paul wrote, "Nevertheless, death reigned from Adam to Moses, even over them that had not sinned in the way that Adam did who was the figure of him that was to come."

Death did what? It reigned. Death reigned from Adam to Moses, and we know Moses brought the law, the Ten Commandments. So we understand more clearly why Job had the experience he had. Job's life fell between Adam and Moses. Although it is not the first book in order, Job is the oldest written book in the Bible. So therefore, if death reigned from Adam to Moses and we know that Job was before Moses therefore in the time in which Job lived, death did reign. The trial that Job went through was not a byproduct of Job, it was a byproduct of the season in which he lived. Because Satan reigned, death had the right.

Some people read that God said, "Have you tested my servant Job," and they wonder how come God threw Job under the bus like that. God did not throw Job under the bus. Moreover God let the devil know that He already knew Satan was looking at Job. God asked because God knew that Satan was about to. What Job went through was a byproduct of that time because death reigned. Then Moses came into the picture, and he brought the Law; if you could live by the Law, you would not experience the effects of sin. (I am simplifying for the purposes of this portion of the book. Please note that there is far more to be expounded on in this area.) Upon Moses' receiving the Law, death no longer reigned, but death still had rights. If you abused the Law, then death had its right in your life.

Since Moses brought the Ten Commandments, people have had a choice. If we follow God's Law, we will not experience the effects that death brings. But if we choose not to do what is right, then the effects of the curse of the Law are allowed to operate in our lives. Two worlds, or two systems, were created when Moses brought the Law. Now a choice exists.

Finally Jesus was incarnated in his earthly ministry knowing that people could not keep the Law perfectly. Many were trying to keep the Law, trying to do what was right of their own volition and ability. Jesus then made the ultimate sacrifice. From the moment He died on the cross and was resurrected and ascended, the effects of the curse of not keeping the Law have been removed. Now we still recognize God's Law because the person who loves Him will still keep His commandments. Now you are mindful that Jesus removed the curse that comes when you make a mistake. Under the Law of Moses, if a person made a mistake and there was no atonement made by the high priests, then that person could not be right with God. Then Jesus came and fulfilled the requirements of the Law and paid the entire price for our eternal redemption and salvation. Now God reigns because Jesus paid the cost.

When Jesus said on the cross, "It is finished," it was finished!

Here is the crux of my point: Since two realms still reign, what are we believers responsible to do? Help people know that they are in that world. Because in that world, nothing ever works the way it is supposed to. "Nevertheless death reigned from Adam to Moses even over them that had not sinned in the way Adam did but who was the figure of that which was to come. But not as the offense so also is the free gift, for if through the offense of one, many are made dead, much more the grace of God and the gift by grace which is in one man, Jesus Christ. So if by one man's offense, Adam, many became dead, then much more the grace of God and that gift by grace which is one man, Jesus Christ, abounded unto many. And not as it was by one that sinned so is the gift; for the judgment was by one to condemnation, but the free gift is of many offenses unto justification, for if by one man's offense death reigned by one, much more which receive abundance of grace of the gift of righteousness shall reign in life by one Jesus Christ."

If death reigned and had the right to do anything, and God said, "Now you reign," then there must have been something that took place to shift the control and the authority from Satan who was reigning, over to Christ who is now reigning. When Christ was resurrected there was a paradigm shift or a power shift that occurred where Satan was in charge! Jesus took control then shifted it over to His people! Paul says, "How much more shall you reign in life?" If by one offense of judgment, condemnation came upon all men, even so by the righteousness of one, a free gift came upon all men in justification of life.

"Who is it that ascended except he descended?" When Jesus ascended to the Father, His ascension seated us in heavenly places; He first descended into the lower parts of hell. Psalm 52 describes what Jesus went through when He descended into hell. We know that He went into hell to take back the keys to the kingdom! When Satan deceived Eve and Eve led Adam astray, Satan took the authority from Adam and Eve. He reigned from Adam to Moses, because he took the authority and dominion from Adam.

Are you with me? If we follow a biblical timeline, we can see that Satan took the authority from Adam. Then later, Moses came along and introduced the Law. The Law brought relief from Satan's reign. Unfortunately, however, it created almost a duel world. If you were able to follow the Law, then you were free from the reign and curses of Satan. But no one could live up to the mandates and ordinances of the Law that required atonement and sacrifices to appease the wrath of God for sin.

Fast-forwarding to the New Testament, Jesus came into history and dealt with this problem forever. He took back man's authority and dominion. Satan still has authority in this world, but he has no authority in the life of a believer. Do you remember when the disciples came to Jesus and they asked why a man had been blind from his birth? "Who sinned?" they asked, because they knew sin causes sickness. They thought they knew that sin was the cause of disease. The question they were asking was, did the blind man sin while he was in his mother's womb, or did his mother and father sin.

Jesus responded and basically let them know that they were asking the wrong question! What they should have been asking is why are we sitting here at this time with this sick individual. Jesus informed them that the man was blind so that the power of God may be made manifest, that people would see the power of God! Because Jesus came to destroy the works of the devil!

So what did Jesus come to do? To destroy the works of the devil! You understand we are dealing with principalities and powers. You understand that we are not of this world; we are merely in this world. You understand now that Satan had rights to this world ... until Jesus took back His rights over us.

According to Colossians 2:14, people no longer have to step through the hoops of Law, but need to have to have a relationship with God through Jesus. And He moved the Law out of the way! In the Amplified version, verse 15 says, "[God] disarmed the principalities and powers that were ranged against us and made a bold display and public example of them, in triumphing over them in Him and in it [the cross]." So the Apostle Paul said that God disarmed them, right? Do you realize that there is a difference between restraining, constraining and detaining? If I strip you of your weaponry, have I stopped you? Have I destroyed you? No. You still could do what you want to do, you just can't use a weapon against me.

No weapon formed against me shall prosper. The Bible does not tell us that the weapon will not be formed. It does not tell us that there will not be a plan formulated. It tells us that it will not prosper. If you understand that, then you realize that Jesus disarmed them, but He did not remove them. So they are still here, disarmed and stripped of their power. This is important because even though we want God to take Satan away from us, His answer is no! Why? Because Jesus already disarmed him! So, what do you do? When your enemy comes at you with what looks like a gun, in reality, it is only his finger in his coat pocket appearing like a weapon. We see what appears to be a gun and freak out. Because sometimes we fail to realize Satan was disarmed! He has no weapon — none! His only weapon against you is to trick you. He is all about deception. He will try to make you think you are going to die.

We have to understand that he has been restrained, he is constrained, but he is not detained.

Revelation 20:1-3

John writes, "And I saw an angel come down from heaven, having the key of the bottomless pit and a great chain in his hand. And he laid hold on the dragon, that old serpent, which is the Devil, and Satan, and bound him a thousand years, and cast him into the bottomless pit, and shut him up, and set a seal upon him, that he should deceive the nations no more, till the thousand years should be fulfilled: and after that he must be loosed a little season."

Jesus did not come and literally detain Satan; He did not lock up Satan. He stripped him of his weapons and authority. Not until the thousand-year millennium when Jesus returns with us, the glorious church, to take back what belongs to us in the establishment of our eternity, only after the tribulation does Satan get bound. Revelation says the angel has the key to the bottomless pit that Satan and everyone who serves him will end up in. Until that happens, he is not *detained*; he is *constrained*. He is running around doing as much damage as he can do. Some people tend to think that Jesus destroyed the devil. No he did not! The Bible tells us that Jesus came to destroy the *works* of the devil. He disarmed him; He stripped him of his power; He took back from him His authority in your life; but He did not lock him in a jail cell! Therefore, Satan is running around doing whatever he wants to do! Then finally, we shall return with Christ to bring judgment upon the world, and that is what is called Armageddon, the final battle! Until the final battle, Satan is still out here and he is loosed and he is doing whatever he wants to do. Jesus disarmed him, but Satan is still here.

Luke 10:17-19

Jesus told those He was sending out, "Behold, I give unto you power to tread on serpents and scorpions, and over all the power of the enemy: and nothing shall by any means hurt you."

Nothing by any means shall hurt me! Nothing! Nada! Zippo! Zilch! Bupkis! There you go. So, He says, behold I have given you power, which we understand to be authority.

Gill's Exposition of the Entire Bible states:

"And he said unto them, ... In order to abate their surprise, and reduce their transport of mind: I beheld Satan as lightning fall from heaven; meaning, that this was no news to him, nor any surprising event, that devils should be cast out of men, and be in a state of subjection; for as he existed as the eternal Son of God before his incarnation, he was present, and saw him and his angels fall from heaven, from their first estate, their habitation of bliss and glory, down to hell, upon their sin and rebellion, as violently, swiftly, and suddenly, as the lightning falls from heaven to earth; and when he sent out these his disciples, as soon as they began their work, and all along in it, he, by his divine omniscience, saw the powers of darkness falling before their ministry and miracles; and he also foresaw how Satan hereafter, in a more conspicuous manner, would fall before the preaching of his Gospel by his apostles, not only in Judea, but especially among the Gentiles, where he, the prince of this world, would be cast down from his throne, and out of his kingdom; so that what they related, as it was what he knew before, it was but little in comparison of what he himself had seen long ago, and of what he foresaw would be; and even he would give them power to do other miraculous works besides these."

Jesus was saying that He came from the One who has more sovereign authority than Satan. And then He says, paraphrasing, "Behold, I give unto you authority and power over all his power because he fell!"

Revelation 1:18

The Apostle John reports the risen Jesus as saying, "I am He that liveth, and was dead; and, behold, I am alive for evermore, Amen; and have the keys of hell and of death."

Jesus was letting John know that He had overcome the grave and had the keys to hell and death! If I walk to your house and take your keys, I can come and go as I want! You can build the biggest wall possible with the biggest gate possible, but it doesn't matter how big or strong it is if I have the key to it.

Matthew 28:18 - 20

"And Jesus came and spake unto them, saying, 'All power is given unto Me in heaven and in earth. Go ye therefore, and teach all nations, baptizing them in the name of the Father, and of the Son, and of the Holy Ghost: Teaching them to observe all things whatsoever I have commanded you: and, lo, I am with you always, even unto the end of the world. Amen.'"

Mark 16:15-18

"And He said to them, 'Go into all the world and preach the gospel to every creature. He who believes and is baptized will be saved; but he who does not believe will be condemned. And these signs will follow those who believe: In My name they will cast out demons; they will speak with new tongues; they will take up serpents; and if they drink anything deadly, it will by no means hurt them; they will lay hands on the sick, and they will recover.'"

Jesus is speaking in these portions of Scripture. He did not say that these signs will follow Me only. Notice they don't say, "In My name, I will cast out devils." He did not say, "I will cast them out," nor "I will deal with them for you." Who did He say is going to do it? Those that believe in His name! Name means character, rank and authority.

Here we come full circle. When we ask the Lord to remove a problem or situation, His response is that all power has been given unto Him and He already gave it to you! Don't keep asking Him to do it; He has already done it! So if you want that devil cast out, then you cast it out in the name of Jesus! Stop asking, "God, how come you won't answer my prayer?" He already answered it 2,000 years ago! It is finished; it is done; it is settled! It is time for you to step up into your authority and realize that all power has been given to you! If you want that devil to leave, tell it to leave! If you want that devil to stop, tell it to stop! If you want that devil to get its hands off your family, tell him, "Take your hands off my family!" You are the one. Jesus did not say, "In my name, I will do it."

Matthew 16:13-19

"When Jesus came into the coasts of Caesarea Philippi, He asked His disciples, saying, 'Whom do men say that I, the Son of man, am?' And they said, 'Some say that Thou art John the Baptist: some, Elias; and others, Jeremias, or one of the prophets.' He saith unto them, 'But whom say ye that I am?' And Simon Peter answered and said, 'Thou art the Christ, the Son of the living God.'

And Jesus answered and said unto him, 'Blessed art thou, Simon Barjona: for flesh and blood hath not revealed it unto thee, but My Father, which is in heaven. And I say also unto thee, That thou art Peter, and upon this rock I will build my church; and the gates of hell shall not prevail against it. And I will give unto thee the keys of the kingdom of heaven: and whatsoever thou shalt bind on earth shall be bound in heaven: and whatsoever thou shalt loose on earth shall be loosed in heaven.'"

Jesus and His disciples arrived at the coast of Caesarea Philippi, and Jesus asked His disciples, "Who do men say that I, the Son of Man, am?" Notice that He said Son of Man, not Son of God. Peter responded with "Some say you're John the Baptist, some say you're Elijah, others Jeremiah or one of the prophets." Jesus then asked Peter who he would say that He is, and Peter answered, "Thou art the Christ, the Son of the living God.'

"Flesh and blood has not revealed it unto you," Jesus responded. In other words, No man told you that! You could not know that by flesh and blood. We do not wrestle against flesh and blood. So you would not have known by natural means, by your own learning or thoughts; it is something that could only be discerned spiritually. Jesus further added, "But my Father, which is in heaven, has revealed that to you." Then he informed Peter that upon this rock will He build His church, and the gates of hell will not prevail against it.

The rock that Jesus was building the church on was not Peter. Jesus changed Peter's name to the Greek word for rock, "Petra," but the rock that Jesus referred to was the revelation that He was the Son of God. So we could paraphrase it as, "Upon the revelation that I am the Son of the living God, upon that rock will I build my church, and the gates of hell will not prevail against it."

Why won't the gates of hell prevail against it? Jesus continued and said, "I will give you the keys." So the gates of hell will not prevail against you because Jesus has given you the key to it!

Jesus continued by saying Satan will not prevail against you because you have the key. Let me tell you what the key is. "Whatever you bind on earth shall be bound in heaven. Whatever you loose on earth shall be loosed in heaven." In other words, what you permit him to do, he has every right to do. If you allow it, he has every right to continue. You might passively sit there asking Satan to stop bothering your family, but it is not until you push back that he responds. Remember the woman who came to the feet of Jesus and asked for healing for her daughter and He replied, "This is not for the dogs." She said, "Yes, but even the dogs get a crumb." As a Christian, you must realize that you have authority over your child. So "Satan," you can demand, "take your hands off my child. I'm not asking you, I'm telling you in the name of Jesus! This is not a discussion, do it right now!"

Then he has to go and he is truly upset that you understand your authority. Never give Satan a command and then say, "I hope that worked." Satan will respond, "Come on guys, back up the van and unpack!" You have got to know your authority, and remain unwavering in it.

John 14:13

"And whatsoever ye shall ask in my name, that will I do, that the Father may be glorified in the Son."

69

I love when the Bible reports Jesus' exact words and we can quote Him directly, because His doctrine can never be refuted. John 16:23-24 says, "Anything you ask in my name." He did not say just to ask the Father. He said to ask in His name. The Greek word for "ask" in John 16 is more closely related to *praying to the Father*. But in John 14:13, the word for "ask" would have been better translated as to *demand or to require*.

Where Jesus says, "I will do it," the actual rendering would be better served as, "I have done it." This is a place where people's theology can get off base. They think, "Well, I can command God!" No, you cannot. "I can command Jesus!" No, you cannot. But you can demand what is rightfully yours. And that is what Jesus was saying: "If you ask anything, if you require anything in my name that I have already done, then now when you command it to happen, you are not telling God what to do, you are commanding Satan to oblige what you have asked for!"

I have seen people worrying, feeling helpless, saying, "My kid is sick." They need to realize that Jesus died on the cross so that sickness can be dealt with permanently! In that finished work, you have the right to take your authority over that situation, because now you are commanding Satan, "Let my child go! Loose my wife! Loose my husband!" You can command him because you have that authority in your house. Always bear in mind that if people want demonic things in their life, we cannot override their will.

Now can you go loose something on somebody whom you don't even know? Unless you have been uninstructed by the Holy Ghost to do so, you can only loose and/or bind what is within your direct realm of authority. Your authority functions only in your sphere. If you have no authority there, then those people have got to deal with their problem.

So guess what you have to do? If you want to help somebody get free, what can you do? Teach! You must teach them! You need to show them some Scripture. Because once they get their authority clear, once they understand it, the next thing you know, they will be talking differently. They won't be saying, "Pray for me!" No, there are some times when individuals are too weak to pray for themselves. Then that is when they need to find somebody who knows how to pray and say, "Pray for me." There are a few people to whom I will divulge what I am going through and ask to pray for me, because I know their prayers are successful. However, if I am in possession of all my faculties at the time and I am not overly stressed beyond my measure, then I understand I have authority and it is time for me to deal with my problem myself.

If I do not understand it, then I need to get into the Word until I do. But people say, "I want God to deal with this thing." God is not going to; He already did. And for people to ask Him to deal with what He has already dealt with means that they believe He did not.

I know He already dealt with it because His Word tells me so. When you read the Gospels — Matthew, Mark, Luke and John — they will tell you Jesus died. They will tell you He was resurrected. They will not tell you why or what His death and resurrection fully mean to you. Then you progress into the epistles — Romans, Ephesians, Colossians, etc. These are letters that were written to the church to tell Jesus' followers why Jesus died and what it means to them. This is why Christians must spend more time in the New Testament than the Old. If you spend a lot of time in the Old Testament, you will get legalistic; you will get flaky. You will begin to think that everybody should burn! Once you get into the New Testament, you can begin to understand, "Wait a minute, Jesus died for me?" And in the process of Him dying, He hung on the cross. When Jesus died, He went into hell. Satan thought he had the right to Jesus. However, Satan violated the lease that he had stolen concerning this earth and all that is in it for he had just crucified the Son of the living God. He had rights to anyone who was with sin, but not to the sinless for there is no punishment for the sinless.

When the Law was instituted by Moses, there was still a separation between God and man. If people were in right standing with God by yearly atonement sacrifices, then Satan had no right in their lives. From a New Testament perspective, we understand that those sacrifices were a type and shadow of our Lord and Savior. So when Satan had Jesus crucified, he thought that he had a right to Jesus. If Satan had known, he would have never done it! Now, though, because Satan has broken his lease, he is forever defeated in the Christian's life and he has no rights to you or your life. His realm of authority is only in the life of the unbeliever.

Ephesians 4 tells us that Jesus first descended then ascended and gave gifts to men. He took from Satan and then gave us the keys and gave us all gifts. All of us have gifts; all of us have a purpose. He distributed to believers the power that Satan once had over them.

According to 1 Timothy 6:13-16, Jesus is the King of kings: "In the sight of God, who gives life to everything, and of Christ Jesus, who while testifying before Pontius Pilate made the good confession, I charge you to keep this command without spot or blame until the appearing of our Lord Jesus Christ, which God will bring about in his own time—God, the blessed and only Ruler, the King of kings and Lord of lords, who alone is immortal and who lives in unapproachable light, whom no one has seen or can see. To Him be honor and might forever. Amen" (NIV).

Furthermore, according to Revelation 17:14, "They will wage war against the Lamb, but the Lamb will triumph over them because He is Lord of lords and King of kings—and with Him will be His called, chosen and faithful followers" (NIV).

After Jesus took Satan's power from him and gave it to the church, as noted in Ephesians 4, He seated believers with Him. So we are now seated in heavenly places at the right hand of the Father. Now. Note that it says far above all principalities and powers! So if you understand that, then you realize that when Jesus is called the "King of kings" in 1 Timothy 6:15, then that makes you a king over whom He is the Supreme King. Make sure you do not forget that. That is important.

If you bind sickness in the name of Jesus, it is bound! It cannot continue on. You may still feel symptoms and think that it is still sticking around. But in some situations, you have just got to stand. After you have done all you know to do, stand! You may still feel some aches and pains, but you are healed. Your physical condition may not have changed yet, I know, but you are still healed. Your child still looks like he or she is strung out, I know, but they are healed. "But ... but," you may say, "this situation doesn't look like it's turning; my bank account doesn't look like it has any money in it!" I know, but it is healed. If you do not realize this, then you will run around waiting for God to do something that He has already done.

All authority has been given to you because Jesus had it, and the last thing He did before He left this Earth was He gave it over to you. Now the question is what are you doing with it? The Bible instructs us to be wise and circumspect as we walk this Earth, looking for opportunities to redeem the time. In other words, you need to look for opportunities where you literally can see the glory of God in your life.

But you must also be able to speak it. Once you have instructions from on high, it is time for you to begin to use your mouth and speak the words of God only. You must not speak things like, "I'm never going to make it; this is not going to work out; I don't know where I'm going to get money..." Stop! At minimum, shut up! God says, beloved, above all else, He wants you to prosper and be in good health even as your soul prospers!

My Bible tells me that if I give, it will cause men to give to me "pressed down, shaken together and running over"! My Bible says that if I honor Him first, if I put Him first, then He will cause my presses to burst with new wine! That is what my Bible tells me, and I think what the Word thinks! By His stripes, I am healed. I am healed from the top of my head to the soles of my feet. As a matter of fact, I have got so much healing in me that if you want some you can have some!

I don't take sides based on my emotions; I side with what I know. And when I know the Word of God, then my authority begins to work. You must realize that Jesus gave you the key, and you can stop calling Him and asking Him to let you in. Reach into your pocket, pull out your set of keys, kick that door in and tell the devil, "Nobody moves, nobody gets hurt!"

Have you ever heard somebody refer to an illness as "my disease"? I don't own any disease; it doesn't belong to me! Listen, here is what I would say: "That disease that the doctor says is in my life. ..." But it is *not mine*, because once I say it is mine, I own it. Now when I want that disease to go, it may seem to say to me, "But ... I'm yours! Don't you love me anymore?" No, I don't love you! I don't love anything about you! As a matter of fact, you have got two seconds to get out of here!

We have to understand our authority; we have to realize that all that Jesus came to do is already done. Once you understand that, then you begin to realize, "That's it!" It is time for you to walk in your authority; it is time for you to grow up; it is time for you to realize that God has given you the keys to the Kingdom.

Chapter Four: In the Name of Jesus

We have been delving deeper into the subject of understanding what your authority is and knowing what your authority is not. We tend to not realize the power or the ability that is vested in us. And when we do not understand that, we struggle greatly with the things that happen in our lives. For this reason, some things concerning the name of Jesus need to be clarified.

We have come to understand, according to Ephesians 6:12, that we do not wrestle against flesh and blood, that the struggles and things that we go through are not based in the people we are dealing with, but on the spiritual powers operating through those people. Spirits are disembodied; in other words, they have no body. In the spiritual realm, we understand that spiritual realities are discerned by spiritual beings.

As a Christian, you understand that you are a three-part being. You are a spirit, who has a soul, and you live in a body. You have the unique privilege of being able to reach into several areas to experience stimuli. You have tactile ability. You can touch something and feel it. One item feels soft; another feels rough; ouch, this hurts. You have those abilities because you have the physical senses. You can taste things; you can smell things; you can touch things. These are all senses related to a physical body. If you had no body, you would not be able to feel those things.

In another part of your being, your soul consists of your mind, will and emotions. You can feel happy, sad, excited, disappointed, frustrated, angry. None of those feelings are spiritual things. They are emotional things. Your soul is able to reach into the world of intellect and emotion and receive stimuli.

Demons cannot experience stimuli in those ways because they do not have bodies. They do not have souls. They are not emotionally attached. Therefore, they cannot experience those things. They more or less live their lives, if I can say it that way, without the benefit of being able to experience two-thirds of the experience human beings can have. Thus, since they cannot do those things on their own, their methodology requires them to try to possess, oppress, depress and obsess every person they can, in order to operate in all of the realms.

As a result, we wrestle against principalities and powers seeking physical and emotional expression. Satan expresses himself through those who are yielded to him. If Satan wants to smile, he will smile through those yielded to him. If Satan wants to cuss everybody out, he will literally express that through people.

I watched a show one night that almost had me in tears. The program depicted little kids who have been diagnosed with Paranoid Schizophrenia/Multiple Personality Disorder and other various mental illnesses. One video showed a little girl probably no more than 8 or 9 months old. She was staring off into the distance like she was watching something, and she kept pointing to it, but nobody else in the room could see it. The videos showed her progress as years passed. At one point, the girl got into an argument with her sister and decided she was going to kill her, and began choking her. This little girl almost killed her sister! She was 5 or 6 years old!

As the show continued, showing these effects, I was thinking, "Do these people go to church? Is there anybody spiritual in their lives?" All the while I thought to myself, "Show me their address or something; show me where they live; I'll charter a plane! Let's go out there and deal with some of this stuff!"

The little girl kept saying, "I hear voices." And she named them all — all the different people that were in her life that nobody could see! The people around her were saying, "Well, you know, we don't know what that is." I do!

Toward the end of the program — and I am not trying to make light of this because I know people in the world struggle — here is what happened. Toward the very end, the mother of this girl said, "I have four more years." At this point, the girl was 13 or 14 years old, and the mother was expressing the idea that she had three of four more years before the girl would turn 18. "Once she's 18, she makes her own decisions, so I have to do something before then."

And I thought, "No, you need to do something before then, before she is accountable for herself and you no longer have authority in her life." Because the moment this girl decides she wants those things, that she likes playing with these "imaginary friends," then there is nothing the parent can do about it. The child

79

becomes of the age where she can accept and direct her own authority. That is not so much a numerical age, but an age of responsibility.

Demonic forces are in operation all the time! And we, the members of Christ's church, are walking around oblivious! Babies and young children, struggling with demonic oppression, seeing demons, having conversations with them! This little girl was playing a game and then all of a sudden she switched the conversation to "I want to get a chain saw and kill my mother." Just in the middle of the conversation! Just a flip! We do not wrestle against flesh and blood! Principalities and powers are at work in our world!

Where does a 7- year-old child come up with the idea of how to get a chainsaw? We struggle in the world where we do not even realize that there are principalities and powers, yet we Christians do not understand devils and demons. They have not died; they do not die.

What can we do if we do not even understand that we truly do not wrestle against flesh and blood? You cannot go beat that out of a child! I don't care how bad she is acting! This is not a natural thing; this is a spiritual thing! The look on her face literally changed — it was obvious when it changed; you could literally see it. One could not help but think *this is real*!

What would you do? If no one ever told you that greater is He that is in you than he that is in the world, what would you do? If no one ever told you that all power has been given unto you and you have been given the keys to the Kingdom, what would you do if this were your child? Most Christians do not even have the type of spiritual understanding to go there. But I am taking you there for one reason and one reason only. I want the body of Christ to wake up. "That the eyes of your understanding would be enlightened, that you may know the hope of His calling"!

We cannot keep turning a blind eye to this type of spiritual reality. On this particular television show, that child spent 297 days of her year in a hospital. That leaves 68 days that she spent out. The program showed her medication bin and it was huge, filled with the medications she was taking — psychotic medication, anti-depressants, all kinds of stuff. This was a little child!

I have determined in my heart that I am going to give Satan as much heaven as he is trying to give me hell. If we as the body of Christ are not going to do it, who will? You have to start asking yourself, if "Somebody Else" won't do it, who will?

All Power Is Given Unto Him

Matthew 28:18-19

"And Jesus came and spake unto them, saying, 'All power is given unto Me in heaven and in earth. Go ye therefore, and teach all nations, baptizing them in the name of the Father, and of the Son, and of the Holy Ghost" (KJV).

Jesus did not say "a little power" or "some power" was given; He said "all power" was given. The Bible is broken down by chapter and verse for us to study. But it is not broken into separate thought processes. In other words, verse 18 flows right into verse 19. Sometimes a person might read a chapter, say chapter five, and then read chapter six and think that the two chapters are about two different things, when often they are not. Chapter five will lead right into chapter six with the same theme, the same subject matter. It is the continuity of the Scripture.

Jesus tells us that all power has been given to Him in heaven and earth. Then He tells us, "Go ye therefore...." *Therefore* means what? That which was there before. Basically Jesus said, all power has been given unto Me, now go. Teach all nations baptizing them in the name of the Father, and the name of the Son, and the name of the Holy Ghost. He verbalizes these ideas connecting them all together, in the name of the Father, Son and the Holy Ghost. Now, He says, all power has been given unto me — Go! This is called the Great Commission.

Certain things are required in order to have power of attorney. Number one, the person who gives power of attorney must be competent. Number two, the person who receives power of attorney must also be competent. So transferring power of attorney requires having two competent parties.

A power of attorney does not have to be written in order to be enforceable. It is still a legal contract even if it is oral. However, most organizations want to have it in writing because that is how they can prove it over the long term. Power of attorney is given when the power and rights of one person are given or vested to another person. A properly executed power of attorney says, "You now can do everything I can do." You now can make decisions on my behalf. You can do things in my name, and all you have to do is sign your name and then put the initials POA, which stand for Power of Attorney.

When Jesus said, "All power has been given unto me — Go," what was He saying? He meant, "Look, I took it back now. All power has been given to Me in heaven and in Earth — Go." You have been commissioned. Go ye therefore and do what?

Teach, baptize in the name of the Father, the name of the Son and the name of the Holy Spirit.

The Greek word for "name" is ONOMA. It means character, rank and authority. So when Jesus said go and baptize them in my name, my *onoma*, He was telling them to go and baptize in the character, rank and authority of God, the character, rank and authority of the Son, and finally the character, rank and authority of the Holy Ghost. Go ye therefore with the power that has been given unto Me, go in that power and teach, preach and baptize. Bring them into the family. Under Whose Power?

Mark 16:16

"He that believeth and is baptized shall be saved; but he that believeth not shall be damned" (KJV).

Mark 16 contains the final set of verses in this Gospel. Mark says, "These signs shall follow them that believe." Do you believe? If so, then Jesus says that in His name you shall they cast out devils, speak with new tongues, take up serpents. We know that taking up serpents is not about dancing with snakes and all that kind of nonsense. By taking up "serpents," Jesus is referring to devils and dealing with demonic things. He continues, "It shall not hurt them, they shall lay hands on the sick and they shall recover."

He is saying that in His character, rank and authority, His followers would do these things. Then He was lifted up, ascended and sat on the right hand of God. When He was done giving them His discharge of authority and power, He vested it in them and said, "Go and do these things and realize that miracles will follow the preaching of the Word, that the signs will confirm the Word."

People are looking for miracles. But we do not chase miracles; we chase the Word, because miracles will follow the Word. Without the Word there will be no miracles, because miracles always confirm what the Word is saying! So Jesus said, "Go and do all these things and realize that My power has been invested in you, and in My name you shall do all these things." And then He stepped back and said, "All right, y'all — peace!" Well, He didn't say it quite that way but that is my artistic license. Then He sat at the right hand of God!

God is on the throne, and His right hand always represents power. In the past in some Catholic schools, if children held their pencil in their left hand to write, the nuns would hit them with rulers and get them to write with their right hand. The left hand was considered a sign of Satan and all this other nonsense. We know that such superstitions are not true, but I want to help you understand where this thought process originated.

So if Jesus ascended after His resurrection, and is now seated on the right hand of God, and the Bible says in Ephesians that He has quickened us together with Him, then we can conclude that the Word is telling us you are sitting there with Him! You now have by right of proxy and power of attorney all that is implied by the words "in my Name"! So what has been vested in you has been the name to which every knee will bow, too.

What Is Rank?

Have you ever heard the saying R.H.I.P? It means "Rank Has Its Privileges." We previously established that, according to 2 Corinthians 12:2, God's throne is in the third heaven. Paul said, "I knew a man in Christ ... such an one caught up to the third heaven."

Paul was speaking of himself being caught up in the third heaven. We concluded that if there is a third heaven, there must be a second and a first. So if Paul was caught up in the third heaven, then that must be where God's throne is — in the third heaven, the highest heaven of all with none higher.

If in His rank, Jesus is seated at the right hand of God, then what could be above Jesus? Nothing! If you are seated with Him, then what else is above you (other than God the Father, Son, and Holy Ghost)? Nothing! He has quickened you together with Him far above principalities and powers. Far above!

Satan puts his hook into people's souls. Spiritually nothing is higher than you (in your position in Christ), but your soul has been trained over the years to rely upon your mind, will and emotions, and your physical body relies upon what is here on this planet. For example, if you stop eating, will you die? Of course. Thereby we can see that the human physical body has a dependency upon what is physically here. This simple illustration also demonstrates why people who struggle with drugs cannot break free from them; they have become flesh-ruled and flesh-dominated.

Christians may speak of spiritual things to some people to whom these spiritual truths sound like nonsense. But God's Word says that the same Spirit that raised Jesus from the dead dwells inside of me. And it shall quicken. That word "quicken" is a form of the Greek word ZOE, which means "the life of God." In other words, it gives me the life of God in my mortal body, which will bring my body into the life of God.

Romans 12:1

"I beseech you therefore, brethren, by the mercies of God, that ye present your bodies a living sacrifice, holy, acceptable unto God, which is your reasonable service."

God's Word tells us that our spirit, soul and body are to be preserved blameless. Your *body*? He means just your spirit, doesn't He? He said your *body* is also to be preserved blameless. He is telling us that we need to make sure that our body is also preserved blameless to the coming of the Lord. When you are born again, neither your body nor your soul is reborn. Your spirit is recreated and you become partakers of a divine nature spiritually. However, your soul still has to be renewed. Romans 12:1 tells us we are responsible to make sure that we present our bodies; in other words, the responsibility to control our flesh is ours as we are quickened or made alive by the same Spirit that raised Jesus from the grave, Who also dwells in us.

Acts 4:10-12

"Be it known unto you all, and to all the people of Israel, that by the name of Jesus Christ of Nazareth, whom ye crucified, whom God raised from the dead, even by Him doth this man stand here before you whole. This is the stone which was set at nought of you builders, which is become the head of the corner. Neither is there salvation in any other: for there is none other name under heaven given among men, whereby we must be saved" (KJV).

Peter is telling the rulers and elders of the Jews that the man who has been healed has been healed by the name of Jesus. There is no other name that shall be named by which any man will be saved. There is no other name! The man standing healed in front of them is proof that there is no other name above this name! They respond that these men are ignorant, unlearned! But they all know that the disciples have been with Jesus! There is no other way they could have this understanding, this assurance, this clarity of who they really are other than the authority of the name of Jesus.

There was no other way the disciples could seem so knowledgeable and bold yet be so formally unlearned — unless they had been with Jesus.

Philippians 2:9

"Wherefore God also hath highly exalted Him, and given Him a name which is above every name" (KJV).

The Word here states that God *has given*, not *will give*. He has given Jesus a highly exalted name, which is above every other name. That means that the name of Jesus stands in rank above every other name.

I have my own personal theory, which is not official doctrine per se. I have observed some people struggling with sickness and illness, who say to me that they do not know what it is. I think to myself, *That is Satan trying not to give it a name, because he knows that if he gives it a name, then we Christians have got a name that is above that name.*

I think about this nameless ploy of Satan's whenever there is something that Christians cannot identify and it goes on and on, and they never can figure out what it is. Scripturally, I do not care if it has a name or not. In Christ, we have been placed far above all powers. But I think people who are under satanic attack become confused when the thing they are dealing with never gets a name.

Christians have to understand that everything has to take a knee to Jesus. My spiritual Father says it this way. When Jesus

87

walks into a situation, everything has to recognize that a greater authority has walked into the room! In ancient monarchies, when a person came before a king, that person was required to bow and kneel before the king. If the king raised his scepter with his right hand, the person was permitted to come forward and speak to him. If the king did not lift his scepter, that was it. No audience was granted. The person could turn around and go on about his business or else be fed to the lions.

Notice the Word says Jesus is seated at the Father's right hand; it also says that every knee shall bow. When a greater authority walks into a room, everyone in the room must bow to the greater authority. Thus when the Bible says that His is a name that is highly exalted above all names then at the name of Jesus every knee shall bow. It follows, then, that if I have power of attorney to use His name, then I am able to operate with the same authority that comes with His character, rank and authority.

That is why we end every prayer with "In the name of Jesus." Some people carry that expression like a rabbit's foot as if it makes them lucky to have it attached to their prayers. No, "in the name of Jesus" does not make you lucky! Every Christian is saved! If you believe in Christ you are saved, but that does not make you victorious. Your salvation alone does not make you victorious. There are people who have lived as saved Christians all their lives getting harassed, tormented, and beat up, struggling with sickness and disease, struggling with poverty and then they die! They die never having known that they have authority to deal with these issues.

Just being saved does not make Christians victorious. For example, people who have children know that their child is, in fact, their child. Their children are their flesh and blood, but that fact alone does not make them well-behaving children does it?

We must understand that positionally being a Christian is one matter, but understanding who you are and then exercising that understanding is another. People have told me they have tried to take authority and it didn't work. That is exactly the problem — they tried. I do not *try* to take my authority because I *alone* do not have any. Jesus has the authority and I know He does. Therefore, when I deal in the authority that Jesus has delegated to me, I know that every knee, every single knee must bow! Every single disease must answer to me! Every single devil in hell must respond! Not because of me, but because of the One I serve, the One whose blood was shed on the cross! They all have to answer to Him! Why? Because He overcame the grave! Hell could not hold Him; the grave could not hold Him; Satan could not stop Him! Therefore, if His name is vested in me, if I have His power of attorney, I don't *try*; I just *do*!

John 14:10-14

"Believest thou not that I am in the Father, and the Father in me? The words that I speak unto you I speak not of Myself: but the Father that dwelleth in Me, He doeth the works. Believe Me that I am in the Father, and the Father in Me: or else believe Me for the very works' sake. Verily, verily, I say unto you, He that believeth on me, the works that I do shall he do also; and greater works than these shall he do; because I go unto my Father. And whatsoever ye shall ask in My name, that will I do, that the Father may be glorified in the Son. If ye shall ask any thing in My name, I will do it."

Notice here Jesus said *he that believes* and *if you ask anything in His name*, He will do it. A better rendering would be that *He has seen to it*. Not that Jesus personally is going to do it, but that the answer to the prayer has been accomplished. Then He says that greater works shall you do; not greater in ability, but greater in number because He said, "I go unto My Father." Why was that so important? Because when He went unto His Father, He did what? He sat down on the right hand of God, which now put Him on the hand of power.

And then He paid the price for you, which meant that now you were made right before God, and now the Holy Spirit can dwell inside you — to wit, now greater works will you do. Jesus was one person, but now you are millions of people who have the ability to believe on Him. And when you believe on Him and you say, "in His name," you are now speaking from the right hand of God, which is where you and He are seated. That is where you speak from, not from your worldly condition! Christian, you have got to stop trying to operate from your earthly condition and start fighting from your position! Your condition means nothing! Victory is about your position.

Then Jesus says, "If you ask anything in my name, I will do it." In other words, "I have seen to it." If you ask anything in my name that I have already conquered, I will make sure it happens. Someone prays, "Father God, please deal with this sickness in my child. I don't want to see it anymore; God help us." There is a difference between that and "In the name of Jesus, I rebuke and bind that sickness right now. I take my authority over it; this is my child! And since this is flesh of my flesh and bone of my bone, I take my authority over it right now in the name of Jesus. Devil, you are cast out right now with all of your minions and sickness

90

and disease. Nothing shall affect this body from the top of his head to the sole of his feet. And I take my authority right now in the name of Jesus; be ye whole!"

What do you think Elisha was saying in 2 kings 6:13-17 when he was sitting on the hill and his servant was saying something like, "We going to go down there and fight all them? It is just the two of us!"

Elisha said, "No, it's not just the two of us!" He said, "God, open his eyes that he might see that there are more that be with us than be with them!" And when he said that, his eyes were opened, and all around him were chariots of fire with angels standing on them going, "Come on! Let's go get 'em!"

Matthew 8:5-10

"And when Jesus was entered into Capernaum, there came unto Him a centurion, beseeching Him, And saying, 'Lord, my servant lieth at home sick of the palsy, grievously tormented.' And Jesus saith unto him, 'I will come and heal him.' The centurion answered and said, 'Lord, I am not worthy that Thou shouldest come under my roof: but speak the word only, and my servant shall be healed. For I am a man under authority, having soldiers under me: and I say to this man, "Go," and he goeth; and to another, "Come," and he cometh; and to my servant, "Do this," and he doeth it. When Jesus heard it, He marveled, and said to them that followed, 'Verily I say unto you, I have not found so great faith, no, not in Israel'" (KJV).

The centurion's servant is not with him. His servant is at home. Is his servant his child? The Bible does not say that he is not, but I believe we can reasonably assume that he is not. This leads to the understanding that you have authority over those that for whom you are responsible.

This man is the centurion's servant, not his child. Jesus said unto him, "I will come and heal him." The centurion answered and said, "Lord I am not worthy that You should come under my roof, but speak the word only and my servant shall be healed." He said to Jesus, "Just speak; I am not worthy for You to have to come to help me. All I know is if you speak the word or if you have spoken the word, you do not have to come to my house. Just speak the word, and my servant will be healed."

Then he explains how he has arrived at that conclusion. "For I am a man under authority. Having soldiers under me, I say to this man, 'Go,' and he goes; to another, 'Come,' he comes. To my servant, 'Do this,' and he does it.'"

When Jesus hears this, He marvels and says to them that are following, "Verily I say unto you I have not found such great faith, no not in Israel." He turns to those who have given their lives to follow Him and He says, "Do you see this? I have not seen such great faith, no not in all of Israel!"

The centurion understands authority. He knows that if he tells a man to go, he goes! If he tells him to come, he comes. Not because the centurion has the power to beat him. He has authority to speak to a soldier under his command and that soldier will obey what he is told to do.

In a similar way, it is by my obedience that I understand that when I say to Satan, "Be gone," he goes by my authority in Jesus and the obedience that he has to have to Jesus! It has nothing to do with me, nothing. Satan is not afraid of you; he is afraid of the One in you.

Do you remember the cartoon "Tom and Jerry" from years past? There was a little dog that always went, "Hey Butch, hey Butch, huh Butch?" The big dog was named Butch. In one episode Butch threw Tom up a greased flagpole, and Butch was teaching the little dog how to take charge and bark and growl at Tom. Tom was not scared of the little dog and made fun of and teased him. But he was deathly afraid of Butch. As the little dog was barking away, and Tom was scrambling up and slipping down this flagpole, Butch was sitting behind him. As long as Butch sat behind him, Tom tried to no avail to climb the pole and get away from the little dog.

You have to understand something: It has nothing to do with you. It has to do with the fact that when Satan looks at you, he sees the One in you. The authority is vested in God's name, and God gives you power of attorney to operate and function in his stead. The centurion was telling Jesus that he knew the Man with the authority did not have to come to his house. He could just speak the word.

When the centurion asked Jesus to heal his servant, Jesus had not yet gone to the cross. He had not yet taken on His back the stripes that would heal us of our diseases. The promise of His servant's healing was in the future. Jesus had not yet crossed over from His earthly ministry to His eternal priestly ministry.

The centurion was not in the same position as Christians are today. He did not have the right to claim healing because Jesus' work on the cross was still in the centurion's future according to earthly time. But when we pray for healing, we are asking for something that has already been accomplished for us in the past — the full redemptive work of the cross. Yet some believers are waiting for Jesus to gain victory over sin and disease and death as if it's in the future. But Jesus has already spoken the word of healing, and according to 1 Peter 2:24, by His stripes we are healed. If He says it, we can have it.

Some people say things like we can just name and claim it. No we cannot just arbitrarily name it and claim it. But if Jesus died for it and He said we could have it, that's a different story. There are 7,000 promises in the Bible; healing is one of them, prosperity is one of them! As believers, we don't need Jesus to heal us; we need our minds to be renewed to receive what He has already done for us. If we stand on what has already been said, then all we have to do is believe and receive.

1 Corinthians 2:6

"Howbeit we speak wisdom among them that are perfect: yet not the wisdom of this world, nor of the princes of this world, that come to nought" (KJV).

The Moffatt's Translation says it this way: "To the dethroned powers who rule this world." They have been dethroned. Their powers have been stripped, so therefore they are dethroned. Then Paul says, "I speak to you in things that are not discernible to those who are young in Christ." They are above the things of the world, but Paul is telling them, what I am saying to you is a higher level of revelation. The wise and the mature get it, but the ones who are young in Christ — the babies — they don't get it. They do not even realize that the world has been dethroned.

So what is the job of mature believers? To help these spiritual babies learn that the world has been dethroned, because there are people who struggle with this. They say, "Do you mean to tell me that all I have to do is take my authority over it?" That's right. "Do you mean to tell me that is all I have ... doctors say this and the world says this ..."

Yes, the world has a system. We still have to operate in it. Don't be stupid and say things like, "I'm not going to take my medicine anymore because pastor said I can take my authority." Take your authority over it, and when you are healed, you can stop taking your medicine. Jesus said, "Go show yourself to the priest," the equivalent of a doctor in His day. In other words, "Go show yourself to them and let them confirm what I did in you." What Jesus does, does not need to be hidden; it will be confirmed by man.

Young people in the Lord do not understand that the world's system is separate from us, the Church. Paul is saying here, that in our world, they are dethroned.

I have no fight with someone who has been dethroned. If the president was impeached from office, and was no longer President of the United States, does he retain the ability to negotiate on behalf of the country? No, because he is not in office. He does not have that authority. He has been "dethroned."

When you understand that Satan has been dethroned, then you understand that the reason why the name of Jesus is so important is because He is the One who dethroned Satan! When you come in the name of Jesus, you are not coming as you, you are coming as the One who sent you!

When Jesus says, "He that receiveth Me receiveth the One who sent Me," He is saying, "If they receive you, they will receive me, and they will receive God because I have vested myself in you! So when you come under My name, My rank and My authority, they do not see you, they see Me!" That is where your authority comes from, because Jesus is the One who dethroned Satan. Jesus said, "I beheld Satan fall like lightning." So when you come to satanic forces in the name of Jesus, you are coming as the One who sent you. Either He is greater, or He is not. Either you are far above or you are not.

Acts 3:1-9

"Now Peter and John went up together into the temple at the hour of prayer, being the ninth hour. And a certain man lame from his mother's womb was carried, whom they laid daily at the gate of the temple which is called Beautiful, to ask alms of them that entered into the temple; who seeing Peter and John about to go into the temple asked an alms. And Peter, fastening his eyes upon him with John, said, 'Look on us.' And he gave heed unto them, expecting to receive something of them. Then Peter said, 'Silver and gold have I none; but such as I have give I thee: In the name of Jesus Christ of Nazareth rise up and walk.' And he took him by the right hand, and lifted him up: and immediately his feet and ankle bones received strength. And he leaping up stood, and walked, and entered with them into the temple, walking, and leaping, and praising God. And all the people saw him walking and praising God" (KJV).

This man expected to receive money. Peter responded that he did not have any silver and gold but what he did have was greater. Sometimes people want things in their life; they want material stuff. They do not realize what they really need is not to get a fish, they need to learn — they need somebody to teach them — how to catch fish for themselves.

This is the point where mature people need to say, "Listen, I'm not going to give you a gift; I'm going to hook you up with the Giver! I'm not going to give you something temporary; silver and gold I do not have. What I do actually have is power of attorney over the Name that can fix your ailment. I am not going to deal with your current need; I am going to deal with what really is going on in your life! Let me introduce you to the One who is the life giver! Let me introduce you to the One who will heal your physical body! Let me introduce you to the One Whose Bible says that His seed will never have to beg for bread! Let me introduce you to Him, the One who is the God of Abraham, Isaac and Jacob! Let me introduce you to Jehovah in the flesh! Let me introduce you to Him!"

And His Word says, "Rise up and walk." Then, the Bible says, Peter took the lame man by the right hand ... which hand? Right hand! And immediately his feet and ankles received strength. And he leaping up stood and walked and then went into church with them. Walking and leaping and praising God because he had gotten more than what he had asked for! And he got it by the name of Jesus!

And he went into church walking and leaping and shouting and screaming because his God was worthy of praise! His God had healed his life! His God had done everything that he asked for and more!

Sometimes people can become so familiar with the blessings of God in their lives that when they get their miracle, it doesn't mean anything to them. I want to tell you something — every time I see God move, I cannot help but get excited. I understand the miraculous power of God. I know that the authority of God has been invested in me — that I have His power of attorney and I get to operate on His behalf. Jesus said that I will do greater works, because He was going to the Father! If you want the world to change, it is time for you to step up and say, "In the name of Jesus, I will not allow corruption to ruin this world! In the name of Jesus, I will not let my child be strung out! In the name of Jesus, my body will be healed! In the name of Jesus, devil, you cannot have this business!" In the name of Jesus, it is time for you to start letting loose and stop sitting back! You have been equipped and empowered to use His name. Vested in you is the power to use His name! So when Satan asks you, why do I have to leave, you can say, "Because, see Him? He said you have got to go. So I'm giving voice to it. Now go! In the name of Jesus."

Why do you need to know this? You need to know it so that you can take your authority. You need to *know* it. Don't *try*. Don't say, "Well I'm going to try that." No, no. The sons of Sceva tried and the demon jumped on them, whopped them, stripped them and sent them running. Don't *try* — do! Realize that we *do*.

My prayer for you is that you begin to truly, literally understand the hope of His calling and the riches of His inheritance in the saints, which He wrought when He raised Christ from the dead. It is not about you waiting for something to happen. You need understanding that it is your responsibility to operate in the character and the rank and authority of Christ. The world is waiting on you. Some of you have businesses in you, and God is waiting on you to act toward establishing them. He has already given you the dream and you think it seems too big. That is how you know it is God. Some of your promotions are waiting on you. For some of you, the only reason why the places where you work are still in business is because you are there.

I am not talking about arrogance; I am talking about confidence! My father would say to me, "I'm not conceited; I'm convinced!" The Bible says, "Cast not away, therefore, your confidence, for it has great recompense of reward." I'm not talking about your faith in you; I'm talking about faith in the One who sent you. I know that everything I put my hands to prospers! It has to, it doesn't have a choice! Not because of me, but because of my God.

Chapter Five: Selection Versus Succession

History helps us develop greater understanding. This concept of *Kingdom* is important to understand when dealing with our authority. The United States of America is a democracy, and as citizens of a democracy, we have a different understanding than the people of biblical times. In those days, leadership was a monarchy, an empire/kingdom or a republic. A republic is a system in which the citizens elect those who will represent them in government. Leaders are chosen by selection and not by succession. Leaders are selected in order to run the country, run the territory of whatever it may be. But leadership is chosen by selection and not by their succession.

In a kingdom, the king of that country is not chosen by selection; he is chosen by succession. The importance of that statement lies in the fact that in a kingdom, the person who is next in line as an heir is *not unaware of that succession*. It is already mandated that there is a successive line based on the bloodline from the present ruler to another person who is the next ruler in line.

By contrast, in a republic, there is a democratic process of selection in which someone is chosen to be leader. When you understand kingdom, then you realize that a democracy represents the will of the people. A kingdom represents the will of the king. So in comparing a kingdom versus a republic, you understand that the citizens of a republic select their leaders based on certain criteria. Are they handsome enough? Do they look the part of the president? Do they act the part of the president? Do they have the education level of a president in order to be selected to govern and rule? Whereas in a kingdom — no matter how intelligent, no matter how skilled or unskilled the firstborn may be — all that matters is that he is the firstborn or in the bloodline of the reigning king!

So when you understand selection versus succession, then you realize that with selection you must have affiliations, you must have popularity. With succession, none of those things are required.

Because we live in a democratic society, I think American Christians do not really understand the concept of kingdom and all that means and encompasses. A kingdom is a king's domain. And a king's domain is the area in which the king rules. As I write today, there are more than 40 kingdoms in the world that are ruled by one monarchy. More than half of them are under the British Empire. That is why the saying goes that the sun never sets on the British Empire — the British have so many territories all around the world that at any given point in time, the sun is shining over land or territory that belongs to the British Empire.

The United States has an embassy in China. Do you realize that the ground on which that embassy sits, wherever those gates are, is U.S. soil? If you are being chased by the Chinese police and you step through that gate, their pursuit must stop. Even though you are within China's borders, you are officially on U.S. soil. Everywhere a nation or kingdom has an embassy, that nation or kingdom is and has control over that plot of land, has authority and influence in it. The embassy belongs to that kingdom regardless of its geographic location.

This is why God told Joshua, "Wherever you put your foot I have given you." You need to understand that you can have territory within another area and be completely separate and different because it is under different rule. Chinese rule does not overstep U.S. territory. Physically the U.S. ambassadors are surrounded by Chinese people and are immersed in that country. They literally may not possess enough physical power to defeat all of China from that location. But the reality is, it is not their location that yields them their power. It is the understanding that their embassy is backed by a powerful nation, and if anything comes against that little postage stamp of land, the national power it represents will release its airborne defense forces to bring into subjection the whole territory coming against it. This despite how small this little parcel of embassy land may be.

We American Christians tend to think in a democratic or a republic style because that is what most of us in the U.S. are used to. However, when you understand kingdom, then Ephesians 6:12 makes more sense: "For we wrestle not against flesh and blood but against principalities, against powers, and against rulers of the darkness of this world, against spiritual wickedness in high places." The word for *ruler* has the same root from which we get *monarchy, someone who rules*. There is a ruler of this world, and he is the one with whom we wrestle. We do not wrestle against flesh and blood; we wrestle against the one who rules this world. The challenge we face as Christians is that we are not *of* this world; we are simply *in* this world, but definitely not of it. There is a difference. You can be a person or a man of the people or you can be a man for the people but that does not make you of that territory.

When Paul made this reference, he was helping us to understand how a kingdom works. American presidents and leaders are not called rulers; they govern for only a set number of years. They are not in their positions for life. Our government does not give us practical experience to understand or equate to the concept of kingship. And one of our challenges is this: Whatever a king spoke became a decree, and it became law the moment he spoke it. Remember when Daniel was thrown into the pit? King Nebuchadnezzar came to see Daniel in the pit because the king regretted the result of his decree, but he could not stop it because he had already decreed it.

I want to change your language just a little bit. Because he decreed it, he came running to the pit the next day looking for Daniel hoping that he was all right. But he was the king! If he was king, why couldn't he go against what he had already decreed? Because when a king decrees something, it is not reversible. It is not revocable. The Word of God has to be the primary source of your life! But sometimes people refuse to listen to the Word of God, because they think His Kingdom is a democracy! It is not a democracy — it is a theocracy! When God said it, that was it!

There is no other! None. When you understand kingdom, you realize that even God is subject to his own rules. It is not a problem for God to decree things, because within Him there is no error, there is no lying, there is no flaw. He already knows He is well capable to comply with that which He decrees. Which is why some people struggle with the idea, *Why doesn't God remove Satan completely?* Because Satan stole the right from us and because God honors the rules he set up. I know this is difficult to believe because we see everything as right and wrong. However, God gives as much honor to Satan as He does to us. Because in Him, there is no flip-flop!

Matthew 11:11-12

"Verily I say unto you, among them that are born of women there hath not risen a greater than John the Baptist: notwithstanding he that is least in the Kingdom of heaven is greater than he. And from the days of John the Baptist until now the Kingdom of heaven suffereth violence, and the violent take it by force."

John the Baptist was charged with the responsibility to prepare the way of the Lord. John's assignment was to declare that the Kingdom of heaven was on its way. His job was to declare and to herald that the Kingdom of heaven was coming! That is why he had been in consecration for thirty-something years in the wilderness in a situation where nothing was supplied! Dryness, barrenness ... Some of you have been in situations where you feel like your life has been barren. John the Baptist was there for thirty years! It was a measure to build him up to prepare him, to get him ready to go forward before the King and say that the Kingdom is coming! The Kingdom is coming! Prepare ye the way! Repent! Get baptized! Realize that the Kingdom of God is at hand! John the Baptist was specifically chosen for that purpose.

He emerged out of the wilderness with camel underwear on! He emerged with honey in one hand, locusts in the other! Mmmm, yummy! Let's put that on the menu. There was something different about him, and the world would have looked at him and said, "What? This guy is wearing leather underwear, eating honey and locusts and he's going to tell me what?"

Here's what: That the Kingdom of God was on its way! The time they had all been waiting for! What you do not understand is that nothing of biblical significance had happened for four hundred years! There is no other information in the Bible for four hundred years from the Old Testament to the New Testament — nothing had occurred. It was dry; it was dead; then here comes this guy out of the wilderness saying, "Hey! Prepare the way of the Lord! Repent! The Kingdom is at hand." That is why Jesus said that there was none greater than John the Baptist, because his job was to herald the coming of The King and His Kingdom.

There came that moment when John was baptizing folks, and he saw Jesus from afar off. Never having met Jesus other than one occasion, he never physically met him, but they were in the womb at the same time when Mary and Elizabeth came into contact with each other, and he jumped in her belly, but he had never laid eyes on Jesus. And now when he sees Him coming, I'm going to say it this way: He senses Him coming! He *knows*, "Wait a minute, there He is! Behold the Lamb of God! The One who has come to take away the sins of the world!"

Then he says that he has to decrease so that Jesus might increase, because this One is coming whose shoes he is not even worthy to tie and whose sandals he is not worthy to wear. He is the One who will bring about the Kingdom. Then here are John's friends asking him if he is okay with people who have been following him leaving and following Christ. John knows that he came so that whoever followed him would eventually follow Jesus. He knows that if they have been following him as he follows Christ, then he will have no problem with them following Jesus. Because Jesus is the One he has been telling everyone about. He does not get jealous or possessive.

Concerning kingdoms, empires and republics, the biggest difference between a kingdom and an empire versus a republic is selection as opposed to succession. However, in an empire the next person in charge is usually not chosen based on succession family-wise; the successor is chosen based on whom the emperor is grooming to take his place. In a kingdom, succession tends to follow the next kinsperson in line. The Queen of England has a next of kin who will be the soon-coming king. There is nothing that can be done to change that succession unless that person dies — in that case, the throne would fall on the next in line.

This is an example of a birthright. This is succession, not selection. As a child, the prince is being groomed to take over and to be in a king's environment. He is being groomed and taught how to act like a king, how to carry himself like a king, how to have kingly manners. He is being taught and groomed this way because the people surrounding him and caring for him know that eventually he will be king. This eventuality is not subject to whether or not someone chooses him; he is.

When an empire takes over territories, it tends to leave the religion intact. The rulers just remove the government. They leave the culture intact. That is what an empire is. If you study Roman history, you will see that every time the Roman Empire became a republic, it grew and it flourished. When it functioned as an empire or a monarchy, if you will, it always struggled with deceit, deception, corruption and problems. And eventually those internal issues would lead ultimately to its demise. Why? Because you cannot successfully take over a territory and maintain it forever without bringing about change in the culture.

Jesus says that the Kingdom of Heaven suffers violence, but the violent take it by force. The Bible tells us to come out and be separate. Then we get a clearer picture that we are not of the world, yet we are in the world. And it is our responsibility to bring change to society. Just as in baking, salt and leaven make significant change to a recipe, so we are to make a difference in the world. But here is what Christians try to do: They try to bring their Christianity to an area of their life without making the change that Christ will always require. So they are accepting of cultures and religions and things that are truly contrary to their Christianity and they say, "But I'm a Christian!" But they are not affecting culture.

This is the difference between a kingdom and an empire. An empire tends to leave a culture intact. "We don't care if you worship Baal, just as long as you pay your taxes." But when you understand kingdom, you can see that a kingdom does not just leave a culture intact. When a kingdom takes over, it begins to change culture. Look at how the United Kingdom impacted India's culture and language. Although the British tried to annex Ireland to the kingdom, Ireland resisted and eventually in the late 1990s won their independence.

How is that possible? Because when the United Kingdom took over in Ireland, they began to try to influence Irish society. So when a kingdom comes in and takes over, the new language that is spoken is kingdom language! Not empire, not republic.

Colossians 1:11-13

"Strengthened with all might, according to His glorious power, unto all patience and longsuffering with joyfulness; giving thanks unto the Father, which hath made us meet to be partakers of the inheritance of the saints in light: Who hath delivered us from the power of darkness, and hath translated us into the kingdom of his dear Son" (KJV).

This portion of Scripture tells us that we were translated into the Kingdom of God's dear Son Jesus.

The King's Domain

If you were translated from darkness into the Kingdom of God, then you understand that there are two kingdoms. And you have been translated from one to the other. You have now defected from one kingdom to another, and your citizenship is now changed. You have left one kingdom; you have applied for citizenship of another kingdom; you have been granted your green card; you are now a legal citizen of this Kingdom of Light and you are forsaking the kingdom of darkness.

It is bizarre how people who are becoming United States citizens have to learn about U.S. history and the Constitution, and how some of those people know more about our country than we do, who have grown up in it. Well, that is because they *desire* something that has a *level of selection* in it. We *have* succession and it has become common to us. One is granted by birthright; the other is a process of choice.

These two kingdoms exist at all times. If you are behaving like you are a citizen of the kingdom of darkness — if you are living in darkness, perpetuating darkness — and you are trying to figure out why light does not come, it is because you are living in the kingdom of darkness. Jesus has translated us from the kingdom of darkness into the Kingdom of Light, which means that we no longer are subject to the ruler of darkness. Whatever he says doesn't mean anything! If the ambassador of China instructed everyone in the world to cut off their right hand, I am quite certain that you would feel that maybe those in China can do that, but he has no authority over here in your house. You would recognize that he has no rule or authority over you, and you would reject his leadership.

Romans 8:15

"For ye have not received the spirit of bondage again to fear; but ye have received the Spirit of adoption, whereby we cry, 'Abba, Father'" (KJV).

Notice that Paul says that you have not received the spirit of bondage "again." The implication here is that we had it at one point. He says, "but you haven't received it again." Why does he say that? Because you must see that you have received the spirit of *adoption*. "Whereby we cry, 'Abba, Father.'" The word *abba* is "daddy." It accentuates the difference between being a father and being a daddy. There are a lot of men who are fathers; they have helped to create a child. But it takes a special man to be daddy; there is a difference.

You have received the spirit of adoption whereby you cry "Daddy God" or "Daddy Father." If you are no longer in the world and you have now been translated into the Kingdom, then the

Apostle is saying that now you get to call God "Daddy." You have not been given a spirit of bondage again, which is a reference to Satan's kingdom. If you are in Satan's kingdom, then you have the spirit of bondage.   Juxtaposing the two kingdoms, Paul is saying that if you belong to God, then you have been given the spirit of adoption; you have been selected. But if you have the kingdom of darkness, you are in bondage. Again, two kingdoms are clashing. He is responding from his position in God's Kingdom against the kingdom of darkness. That is why Paul continually refers to the idea of kingdoms. Kingdom of Heaven, Kingdom of God — they are the same thing. He wants to let people know that where he speaks from is not from the kingdom of darkness — he is coming from his position in the Kingdom of Heaven — truly he is coming from a whole different world. That is why the Bible calls Christians aliens! Believers in Christ are pilgrims; you are not from this world! You are not *of* this world; you are merely *in* it.

Paul continues in verse 16, "The Spirit itself bears witness with our spirit that we are the children of God. And if children, then..." Heirs of what? "And joint heirs" with whom? Jesus! "If so be that we suffer with him that we then may be glorified together." Remember the Bible says we were quickened together and seated in high places with Christ. Quickened together with, far above principalities, far above powers, far above might, far above dominion. The Spirit within us bears witness with our spirit that we are not just people who know God; we are children of God. And if we are children, then we are heirs of God! And in case you did not know, we are now joint heirs with Christ!

Galatians 3:29

"And if ye be Christ's, then are ye Abraham's seed, and heirs according to the promise."

If you are in Christ, then you are Abraham's seed and if you are Abraham's seed, then you are an heir.

Matthew 12:22-32

"Then was brought unto him one possessed with a devil, blind, and dumb: and he healed him, insomuch that the blind and dumb both spake and saw. And all the people were amazed, and said, 'Is not this the son of David?' But when the Pharisees heard it, they said, 'This fellow doth not cast out devils, but by Beelzebub the prince of the devils. ' And Jesus knew their thoughts, and said unto them, 'Every kingdom divided against itself is brought to desolation; and every city or house divided against itself shall not stand: And if Satan cast out Satan, he is divided against himself; how shall then his kingdom stand? And if I by Beelzebub cast out devils, by whom do your children cast them out? Therefore they shall be your judges. But if I cast out devils by the Spirit of God, then the Kingdom of God is come unto you. Or else how can one enter into a strong man's house, and spoil his goods, except he first bind the strong man? And then he will spoil his house. He that is not with me is against me; and he that gathereth not with me scattereth abroad. Wherefore I say unto you, 'All manner of sin and blasphemy shall be forgiven unto men: but the blasphemy against the Holy Ghost shall not be forgiven unto men. And whosoever speaketh a word against the Son of man, it shall be forgiven him: but whosoever speaketh against the Holy Ghost, it shall not be forgiven him, neither in this world, neither in the world to come'" (KJV).

Succession Versus Selection

There is an importance to these terms because succession is based on birthright, and selection is based on popularity. Selection is conditional; birthright is unconditional. In terms of a kingdom, all that is required of a successor is that he or she be physically born to the right parents.

The Pharisees accused Jesus of casting out devils by the name and power of Beelzebub, the prince of the devils. In other words, they reasoned that Jesus was able to cast out these devils is because he was also one. And Jesus knew their thoughts and said to them, "Every kingdom divided against itself is brought to desolation and every city or house divided against itself shall not stand. And if Satan cast out Satan, he is divided against himself, how then shall his kingdom stand?" Whose kingdom? Satan's! Jesus went on to say, "But if I cast out devils by the Spirit of God, then the Kingdom of God has come unto you. Or else, how can one enter into a strong man's house and spoil his goods? ..." In other words, take his stuff. Except that that person first binds the strong man, then he will take all of his stuff. Jesus said that a kingdom divided against itself shall not stand. Whose kingdom was he talking about? He was not talking about the Kingdom of God. He was referring to Satan's kingdom.

Jesus was saying that Satan's kingdom is not divided. If you want to find division, come to the church. Church folks are the ones who are divided. "I don't like the music." "I don't like this." "Pastor always says this." "Pastor is always challenging me." "I don't really want to hear the Word, I just want to hide. I want to disappear into the church so nobody knows whether I'm there or not there." "I don't want to be accountable..." If you want to find division, you have to come to God's people.

Jesus went to cast the devils out of the madman of Gadara, and He said, "Who are you?" They did not all step up to fight; one stepped forward and said, "We are Legion for we are many." They were not arguing amongst themselves saying, "You got to talk last time! Step back! Let me talk! Hey I want to talk! It's my turn! You know you did it the last three times in a row!" No, they did not do that! Jesus said, "Who are you?" And one of them replied, "We are Legion, for we are many." Why? Because they understood rank, file and authority and they understand kingdom.

So then, Paul says, "How can anybody be bound and spoiled unless you first bind the strong man?" The Pharisees believed that the deliverance they saw was the effect of Satan's kingdom at work. Jesus told them that it was not Satan's kingdom they were witnessing, and if they saw deliverance, then they saw the power of God.

If you see something that manifests from God, then know this —the Kingdom of God has just come upon you! So where is the Kingdom? Jesus said it is in us! He said if anything like this happens — in other words, if you see a miracle —then know that Jesus has bound the strong man and He has spoiled him. The only way He can spoil it is to bind the strong man. In other words, there is no power that is greater than Jesus' power, so when He walks into the strong man's house, the first thing he does is to bind the strong man. That strong man has no right anymore.

Now this is important because here is what happens: Some of you have got strong men in your life. For some it is poverty, lack, or stinkin' thinkin'. And you won't bind the strong man, which is why you cannot take his stuff! The truth of the matter is he is already bound and Jesus has already conquered him.

114

Jesus cast out devils by the Spirit of God then the Kingdom of God came upon them. We understand that the Spirit of God is inside us. You can speak against the Son of Man and will be forgiven. But you cannot speak against the Holy Spirit for it is the unpardonable sin. Why? Because the Holy Spirit is the embodiment of the Kingdom of God! You cannot come against the Kingdom, God's whole domain, the whole purpose, the whole idea, the whole reason, the whole purpose for being, the whole existence of everything for which God bringing His Kingdom here. You can come against the Son of Man, but don't come against the Kingdom of God. Because if you see anything that is done by the Spirit of God, then you can know that the Kingdom has come upon you.

Kingdom is based on succession, not selection. You can adopt a child, and the benefit of that adoption is you have a choice. You can have children through natural means and you do not get to choose. You get what you get. It is almost a lottery. But when you adopt a child, you are choosing that one! There is a difference — that child was selected. And once he or she has been adopted, that child now has become an heir! So now this adopted child has selection and succession! You, as an adopted spiritual child of God, have become joint heirs with Christ, and if he is the King of kings, that makes you a king by your position. You have been chosen, and succession by birthright is your inheritance as you are part of the Kingdom! Now when your Kingdom is moving, when the Kingdom of God is advancing, then the violent will take it by force! Why? Because you are not a part of the kingdom of darkness! You are a part of the Kingdom of Light! You are a joint heir! You are a child of the King! You are literally a king! That is why your authority works when you work it!

You are not in Satan's kingdom. You have been selected and now you also have succession. As the heir, that puts you in line for the throne. In order for the next in line to become king, the current king must die. Therefore, when the King of kings laid his life down on the cross, He died so that you would be moved into position! Glory to God! Now you have been quickened together with Him! You have gone straight from the pit to the palace!

This is life changing — it really is. You do not have authority over God. He is the King of kings. But you must understand that if you have a Kingdom, the King's domain, whatever occurs in the King's domain is under the King's authority. Now the trick that Satan keeps throwing at you is to get you to think that you are in foreign territory.

If Satan can trick you into believing that you are on foreign soil, then he thinks he can do whatever he wants to you. But you must understand something: As an American citizen, if I travel overseas somewhere to another foreign country and I get into trouble, depending on the news coverage, I may get help, I may not. Unfortunately there are plenty of people who have been left in other countries to die. But if I am a foreign ambassador or a United States senator and I go over to another country and somebody attacks me, it is not simply a crime anymore; it becomes an international incident.

Now as an ambassador —which by the way, is what the Bible calls Christians, ambassadors of Christ —whether I am on my territory or not (because the Bible says everywhere I put my foot is my territory, because the Kingdom of God is within me), anything that happens to me is an attack against the Kingdom of God. God told Joshua that everywhere he placed his foot belonged to him. Likewise, everywhere I go, if I am attacked for any reason, the attack is not merely against me. It is not just a crime; it is an international incident! And if it is an attack against the Kingdom of God, then all hell has to bow to the greater Kingdom!

You understand that an empire will take over territories, leaving their religion and culture in place. If they all go to hell, the rulers of empires don't care. All they want is their money and their land and to take their women and children. We are all waiting for the true empire to come when all will bow to the Christ. Although the Kingdom is on Earth, because it is in us, we are tasked with the responsibility to make a difference. We are taking the culture and resources for God.

Finally here is what I want you to understand: It is not just selection and it is not just succession. You have authority because of both. You have been selected by God and adopted. By your adoption you were made a child thusly becoming an heir. It is your heritage and your birthright to walk in the authority of the Kingdom because of selection and succession.

Chapter Six: The Enemy of Your Soul

Satan's Strategies

It is important to understand not to glorify Satan's ability but to expose his methodology. Previous chapters have made clear who we are as Christians in terms of our authority and our position in Christ as opposed to the conditions in which we sometimes live. While it is good to know how to exercise our authority, I also believe it is equally important to know how to mitigate Satan's opportunities in our life.

Every successful war plan has within it an "evade and escape" plan. Something that is seldom discussed in the church is how to recognize and neutralize or deflect the strategies and the plans that Satan uses against you. People are sometimes oblivious of the damage Satan is doing in their life. The greatest trick, if you will, that Satan has in his little bag of tricks is to convince you that he does not exist. And here is the sad part: There are people involved at various levels of the church who are being used by Satan and do not even know it. They are just not aware. In their personal lives, they are struggling with trying to get the victory in certain areas and they cannot, because they are yielded to the plan of Satan.

As Christians, we are faced with the challenge that we must understand that we cannot allow Satan into our lives in any way, shape or form. There must be a strategy that he uses in order to deceive us, because Satan cannot directly touch you in any way without permission. If he puts his hand upon you, if he puts sickness upon you, if he does anything to you, he is out of order. There are rules to how God set up all of this, and as those rules are the Kingdom rules, we must resign ourselves to the fact that Satan has a plan. He has a very well thought out, detailed plan that he is executing and waging against you. Now the question is, do you know what the plan is?

Some people do not. In the movie *The Matrix* there is a scene in which the lead character, Neo, is having a discussion about whether or not he wants to see the real world. He is offered to choose between a red pill or a blue pill. If he takes the blue pill, he can go back to sleep and act as if he never heard of the artificial reality of life within the Matrix. If he chooses the red one, his guides will show him the truth and "just how far this rabbit hole goes." Some people would rather ignore the responsibility of knowing the truth and go back to sleep, because it is too disturbing to walk circumspectly with their own lives. This is why any church that will preach the Word, uncompromised, is going to get attacked for the Word's sake.

In ancient war tactics, sometimes the last thing they would do was to bring out the elephants. The reason they did not send in the elephants first was because the elephants would trample *everything*. The mere sight of them would instill fear and cause man and beast to flee with terror or face being crushed. The reason why it was saved till last is because the first goal was to take over the territory and seize everything in it. A commander would not want to send out too much of a force to destroy, because then there would be no spoils of war left over. A conquering army would want to be able to use those resources to continue to advance. Their first goal would be to go in and do the least amount of damage possible but to usurp the authority, to take control. Then they could use the conquered nation's resources to keep moving forward.

Think how difficult it would be for foreign conquerors to bring in new supplies all the way from their homeland. If they could simply invade and take over what was there and use the conquered peoples' resources, that strategy would be optimal. Likewise, Satan does the exact same thing. His first goal is not to destroy; it is to utilize you. It is to get you to spend your money on alcohol instead of tithing. He wants you to take your resources and waste them for his kingdom. His strategy sometimes is so subtle that by the time it is exposed in a believer's life, it is too late.

Satan creates ways to utilize your resources and your time. Instead of being involved in activities and programs at the church, people are involved in the things of the world. Satan gets believers to spend their time in things that are not relevant to God's plan and purpose. Then the believer becomes what we call "busy." B-U-S-Y — Being Under Satan's Yoke. The devil seeks to occupy your time, your money, and your talent. Someone may be a talented administrator, so he or she will go work for a major company and be their administrator, but that person won't administrate in the house of God.

Time, treasure and talent are what you have to bring before God. You have time; you have treasure (finances and possessions); and you have talent (your skill sets and abilities). Satan tries to occupy those things, to keep your time and money tied up. When people struggle with their finances, the first thing I ask them is "Are you tithing?" What else can I say? There is nothing else I can say, because the blessing of the Lord is what maketh rich! If a Christian person doesn't trust God in their finances, then when all hell breaks loose in their life, what else can I preach to them? I only have one gospel; I do not know another one. I know only one — it is Jesus.

Satan attacks your time, your treasure and your talent. Why use your skill set for church when you can take it to the workplace? So off you go to the workplace and you work there 70, 80, 90 hours and then you complain when someone asks you to serve for 15 extra minutes in the church. The attack has been waged on the church and there is a strategy and the strategy is to cause you to lose focus. The difference between a light bulb and a laser is one word — focus! A laser is focused light. Energy flows where focus goes.

So here we are, understanding that Ephesians 6 tells us that we wrestle not against flesh and blood, but against principalities and powers and spiritual wickedness in high places. There is a strategy that Satan has used to wage war against us.

Cicero said, "Diseases of the soul are more numerous than those of the body." The attack in your life will tend to originate in your soul. When Satan seeks to create a problem in your life, he is trying to gain an advantage over you. He does not seek immediately to control you in terms of your destruction, but to influence you to be used for his purpose. Like the ancient conquering armies, the last thing he does is release the elephants. Once he has decided that you are no longer willing to yield to what he wants you to do, he can then choose to just level the whole thing.

I submit to you that there are many people right now upon whom Satan has released the elephants. These people have made a decision: "I will not back down; I will not let up; I will not go backwards; I will not refute God; I will stay where I have been planted." Once you have taken that position, that is when Satan says, "Okay, let's get out the elephants and let's just level the place." Here is what happens now because you are this Christian and you are trying to stand. You look up to see that herd charging at you and those things are huge! And they have got tusks on them and they are coming right at you, but you have to realize one thing. God would not let that happen unless He was about to do something in your life! Understand that the reason why the attack is there is because you have stood against principalities and powers!

Nobody wants to take a position anymore. Most people just want to operate within their will. "I want to do this, I want to do that." Listen, "I want to" died in me a long time ago.

I am not sharing this to glorify Satan's ability. I am trying to expose his methodology. He has a methodology — if you do not catch his methodology, you will find yourself on the wrong end of the discussion then wonder how you got there.

2 Corinthians 10:3

"For though we walk in the flesh, we do not war after the flesh: (For the weapons of our warfare are not carnal, but mighty through God to the pulling down of strongholds;) Casting down imaginations, and every high thing that exalteth itself against the knowledge of God, and bringing into captivity every thought to the obedience of Christ" (KJV).

The ESV puts it this way: "We destroy arguments and every lofty opinion raised against the knowledge of God, and take every thought captive to obey Christ." We wrestle not against flesh and blood, right? So this Scripture is saying that the weapons of our warfare are not carnal. In other words, they are not fleshly; they are mighty through God to the pulling down of strongholds. What is a stronghold? A stronghold is an argument or an opinion that has set itself strongly in your mind.

There are good strongholds and there are bad ones. You may have a daughter who is hardheaded and stubborn toward you. However, if she ever finds herself in the back seat of a car, you hope that the good strongholds of her thinking will prevail against the onslaught of some young man's advances. There are good strongholds and bad ones. The bad strongholds are the ones that exalt themselves against the knowledge of God.

Satan seeks to influence and that is the first tactic he uses. His influence comes through an opinion or an argument. It seeks to separate you from others and from God. The whole point of having that opinion or that argument is so that your opinion goes against the Word of God. Once your opinion goes against the Word of God, then Satan has a stronghold in your life, which he now uses as an anchor in your soul. Ephesians tells us to give no place to the devil. Why does it say give no place? Because if you allow the devil in with an opinion, with an argument, you have to ask yourself, "What does the Word of God say?" If you don't know, then don't come back until you know. If the Word of God always prevails in your life then you will always be successful.

Whenever I am faced with opinions and criticism, I always ask myself, "Are they right?" If they are right, then I have got to do something about it don't I? People in today's world have learned to placate themselves by not acknowledging what is right but by doing what feels good. Most people don't want to hear what's right; they just want to hear what feels good. They tend to not want people questioning them and or telling them what to do.

I have been told what to do all my life. I am being told what to do right now. And if you cannot follow people whom you can see, you cannot follow the God you cannot see. Satan seeks to create influence in your life through thoughts and suggestions that contradict the Word of God so that you will believe them. Thessalonians tells us that there were those that refused the truth and God sent strong delusions so that they would permanently believe a lie!

Satan seeks to influence through your mind, your will and your emotions. He begins to get you to dwell on things that you really should not dwell on. He begins to get you to think about stuff that is just not important. He seeks to create things in your mind, in your thoughts. There are floating masses of thoughts, suggestions and opinions that are always floating around. If you want to be successful, you had better learn how to keep your mind and guard it with all diligence. Every thought that comes into your mind that is not of God needs to be cast down. Jesus said, "My sheep know my voice and the voice of a stranger they shall not follow." It is so important for you to know that the first weapon that he wages against you is influence!

Most people think leadership is position. Leadership has nothing to do with position; it has to do with influence. That is what leadership is. If you are out leading and nobody is following you, then you are really just taking a walk. You are not leading anybody. Influence is the very nature of having an effect on somebody. And when you have an *affect* on them, you can then create an *effect* in them. You cannot have one without the other. So Satan's influence comes through your mind.

The second area the devil always comes to influence has to do with environment and associations. If you struggle with alcohol, you should not be hanging in a bar. The Bible tells us that those who are spiritual restore one another, for if a brother falls, those who are spiritual are to restore that brother. The requirement is that the one who is spiritually strong needs to do it lest he stumble over the same sin of the fallen brother. Why? Because Satan is encamped about them with much demonic oppression and activity, in order to cause them to stumble. If you are going to walk into spiritual warfare with this person who is struggling for his or her life, you better make sure you do not struggle with the same thing. Now instead of ministering to them, they are ministering to you! Your environment is absolutely important.

Mark 5:6-10

"But when he saw Jesus afar off, he ran and worshipped him, and cried with a loud voice, and said, 'What have I to do with thee, Jesus, thou Son of the Most High God? I adjure thee by God, that thou torment me not.' For He said unto him, 'Come out of the

126

man, thou unclean spirit.' And He asked him, 'What is thy name?' And he answered, saying, 'My name is Legion: for we are many.' And he besought Him much that he would not send them away out of the country.

This is not the man in the grip of demonism speaking; this man has never met Jesus before. He sees Jesus coming from afar off; he runs up to Him and calls Him Jesus, son of the Most High God. Notice he knows His name and he knows His rank yet this man has never met Jesus before. They then ask if Jesus is there to deal with them before their *time*. What *time*? They are perfectly aware that their time is coming; however, they are reasonably sure that this moment is not it. They understand that they have had a lease on this world. They understand their time is limited. Jesus commands them to come out of the man. Then Jesus asks the man, "What is your name?" And the demons respond, "My name is Legion, (that is, six thousand) because there are many of us." And he begs Jesus not to cast them out of the territory.

He begged Jesus to do what? So wait a minute — he didn't ask Him not to cast them out of the man? So we understand that these thousands of demons were willing to let go of the man, but they were not willing to let go of the environment, or shall we say, territory. This is why we have to be clear about how we interact with our associations and our environments, because I assure you I have never met anyone who has gotten strung out on drugs who did not have drug friends. There is nobody sitting all by himself who just decided, "I am going to produce some crack and smoke it!" See, your environment and your associations will always affect how you are influenced. In other words, when you are hanging around with chickens, you begin to cluck. And as you begin to cluck, suddenly eagles no longer understand the language you are speaking, because now you are clucking instead of soaring. Your environment and your associations mean everything. I am sure you are familiar with the saying "Birds of a feather flock together," or "You can tell who a man is by the friends he keeps." So if you are going to break free from anything, you must change the people, places and things surrounding your life.

This is why people stay carnal. Do you know what a carnal Christian is? It is a person who is saved by having confessed Jesus as his or her Lord and Savior, but he or she has not changed. This person is still carnal. This person still thinks like a baby and acts like a baby. If he doesn't get his way, he stops showing up, he takes his ball and he goes home. But the problem is that the saving of his soul, the saving of her soul occurs through the regeneration process that takes him and her from carnality to spirituality.

Furthermore, to remain carnal is death the Bible says! God expects us to develop because He has a plan for us. Satan expects us not to develop because he has a plan for us. If he can control your environment and your associations then he can control you. This is why when you begin to pursue the things of God then people start to come after you. These people are complaining that the relationship is changing and they are mad because the dynamic is changing! It is changing because the paradigm is shifting. Now Jesus is becoming Lord instead of these people in your life! "So why don't you want to spend time with me?" they ask you.

"No, I never said I didn't want to spend time with you," you say, "but why do you refuse to come to church with me?" These old associations are willing to go with you and do anything else, but those things are a direct assault against God!

Mark 3:31-35 shows Jesus inside a house healing people. When people came inside and told Jesus that His mother was looking for him, He responded with the question, "Who is my mother?" He began to tell them that His focus was to do what His father sent Him to do. It is amazing the level of focus that He was able to maintain. Jesus also said, "He who leaves mother, father, wife, house..." He said, "I will return unto them a hundred times."

Jesus also told us to think not that He came to bring peace, but to separate. Sometimes, if we are not careful, we can begin to think life is all about us! It has nothing to do with you! It has to do with Him! Some things you have got to sever from your life because those things will keep crying, they will keep pulling, they will keep asking, they will keep whining and they will put you in places that you should not be! The next thing you know, you will be *working* in the bar. "Well, I have got to make a living" is your explanation. That is the problem — *you* are making a living and God is not making it for you.

Let me make sure you understand that association always breeds imitation. And people say imitation is the sincerest form of flattery, which is probably true. What is influencing you? I guarantee you, if you are around people who like to party all the time, their behavior will rub off on you. Then suddenly these people who have started partying will wonder, "Why do I have to do all this constricting church stuff when I could be out partying?" By association with those kinds of people, they are influenced to opt for what seems to be more fun for them instead of doing the work that God has called them to do. Never underestimate the subtleties of your environment. This is why people will sometimes wonder why you don't want to hang out with them. It is not that you think you are better than anybody, but the truth is that there are some people you cannot hang out with anymore. They are just too carnal! Every joke will go too far; everything will take on a whole different spin.

1 Corinthians 15:33

"Be not deceived, evil communication corrupts good manners" (KJV).

The ISV version says this: "Wicked friends lead to evil ends." The world is always pulling toward the things and ways of the world. You have to be very careful because you will do some things thinking that you are doing the right thing. But in reality Satan is trying to press you out of your measure. The reality of faith is this: You must understand that you have a measure. And Satan, if he cannot get you to stop operating in faith, will get you to operate beyond your measure. Because once you operate beyond your measure, you are not able to get into faith. So, if he cannot stop you from operating in faith then his strategy becomes to overdraw and bankrupt it.

What is bankruptcy? Bankrupting something is when you try to pull out more than what it contains. Satan tries to deplete your tank; in other words, to take everything from it and take it down to zero. But then if he cannot do that, if you actually stay in church, you stay in the right church, the one that God has sent you to, then your tank keeps getting filled up by that annoying preacher who keeps preaching the Word! Then Satan says, "Okay, I can't deplete their tank, so I'm going to bankrupt it. I'm going to get them to make a demand that is more than what is in it."

1 Peter 5:8

"Be sober, be vigilant; because your adversary the devil, as a roaring lion, walketh about, seeking whom he may devour" (KJV).

Being *sober* means to avoid the drunkenness of your senses, and to be *vigilant* means to be awake. Your adversary the devil as a roaring lion walks about seeking whom he may devour. In that verse, Peter says, "may devour." *May* is a request for permission, not a question of ability.

If I ask you, "Can I play that guitar?" The reality is that you may not know if I can. But if I say, "May I," then I am asking you for permission to play it. The Word says that the devil "may" devour. I am trying to tell you that everything we go through in life is a byproduct of what we permit and what we bind. Accordingly, there are things that happen in my life that I have permitted. Some people may get this twisted because they think *I never told Satan he could do this to me*! You did not tell him he couldn't either. Sometimes silent acquiescence is compliance. To silently acquiesce to something means you comply with it. If you do something in my house and I do not say something to contradict you, then that implies I agree with you whether I do or not. So then we understand that if the devil is roaming around and he is always looking for an opportunity to come into your life and that is where permission has to be given, that is this third strategy that he uses. He tries to get permission from you because permission gives him license. If he has no permission, he cannot function nor operate.

Luke 13:10-17

"And He was teaching in one of the synagogues on the Sabbath. And, behold, there was a woman which had a spirit of infirmity eighteen years, and was bowed together, and could in no

131

wise lift up herself. And when Jesus saw her, He called her to Him, and said unto her, 'Woman, thou art loosed from thine infirmity.' And He laid His hands on her: and immediately she was made straight, and glorified God. And the ruler of the synagogue answered with indignation, because that Jesus had healed on the Sabbath day, and said unto the people, 'There are six days in which men ought to work: in them therefore come and be healed, and not on the Sabbath day.' The Lord then answered him, and said, 'Thou hypocrite, doth not each one of you on the Sabbath loose his ox or his ass from the stall, and lead him away to watering? And ought not this woman, being a daughter of Abraham, whom Satan hath bound, lo, these eighteen years, be loosed from this bond on the Sabbath day?' And when He had said these things, all his adversaries were ashamed: and all the people rejoiced for all the glorious things that were done by Him."

So here the Word says that this woman has an infirmity, sickness of her back, she has been bowed over and has got back problems. Jesus calls her "daughter of Abraham." Jesus tells her, "Woman thou art loosed." She is freed from her infirmity, straightens up, is healed and the religious people say, "Wait a minute! You shouldn't have done that on the Sabbath day." Then Jesus says, "What do you mean? If you had an ox that was tied to a wall and you needed to water it, wouldn't you loose it and give it water? So how much more if you are willing to do this for an ox, shouldn't this woman, who is the daughter of Abraham, be loosed from this condition?"

The term "daughter of Abraham" means that this woman was born a Jew and her ancestors were Jews, that she was a covenant child. Jews by bloodline are heirs of the covenant. That covenant is with them. What allows the covenant to come upon the

Gentiles, the Bible tells us, is that Jesus died on the cross so that the blessing of Abraham might come upon the Gentiles. But she, being born a Jew, was already in covenant. She did not need Jesus to die, per se, because she was already in covenant. So when He came to loose her, all He really brought was the understanding that, *woman, thou art loosed from it!* And He laid his hands upon her and she was loosed from it. Now here is my point: If she was a covenant woman, why was she sick? Because she allowed it. Lazarus was a covenant man — he was Jew. Yet he died with sickness.

Satan tries to get you to permit his plans. There is an experiment where you take a frog and you put it in a pot of water. Then if you turn the heat up gradually, the frog's body will adjust to the temperature and it will eventually get cooked. It will die in that water. Frog soup! However, if you turn the heat up in the water, get it boiling and then you toss the frog in there, that frog literally will hit the water and jump out because it is too hot. Well, I suggest to you that sometimes as Christians we find ourselves in stuff that we would rather just adjust to than to stand against. And we tolerate and permit stuff that happens in our lives that we should be unwilling to tolerate. Because we tend to allow things entrance, sometimes by the time we recognize what is happening, it can be too late.

The final scheme Satan tries to use is offense. If you look up the word *offense,* it means "an act of stumbling." Remember Jesus told Peter that he was an offense unto him. Peter was thinking that he was going to protect Jesus. Jesus told him that he was a stumbling block. In other words, the Lord was telling Peter that if he tried to prevent all of this from happening, he was going to be a stumbling block to Jesus. Because Peter was not looking at the plan of God; he was looking at the plan of Satan.

In order to walk in offense, you must be yielded to the plan of Satan. That is why Jesus said, "You are an offense unto Me; you are a stumbling block." The purpose of offense is it causes its opponent to stumble. It gets you to trip up. If you are running track, you cannot be stumbling. You have got to have your feet moving; you cannot be looking down at them; you need to know that they are down there and moving in sync. As you run your race, remember, Paul said, "I have finished my race; I have finished the course; I have kept the faith." If you are going to run at the speed at which God needs you to move, you cannot yield to offense. Because the moment offense comes, it will cut off your heart because you are now stumbling. And now when you are stumbling you are tripping over things that you should not trip over! "Well, I don't like how Pastor didn't smile at me when he came in today." Really? Are we going to let that define us? Are we going to let that steal everything from us?

Mark 4:10-20

"And when He was alone, they that were about Him with the twelve asked of Him the parable. And He said unto them, 'Unto you it is given to know the mystery of the Kingdom of God: but unto them that are without, all these things are done in parables: that seeing they may see, and not perceive; and hearing they may hear, and not understand; lest at any time they should be converted, and their sins should be forgiven them.' And he said unto them, 'Know ye not this parable? And how then will ye know all parables? The sower soweth the Word. And these are they by the wayside, where the Word is sown; but when they have heard,

Satan cometh immediately, and taketh away the Word that was sown in their hearts. And these are they likewise which are sown on stony ground; who, when they have heard the Word, immediately receive it with gladness; and have no root in themselves, and so endure but for a time: afterward, when affliction or persecution ariseth for the Word's sake, immediately they are offended. And these are they which are sown among thorns; such as hear the Word, and the cares of this world, and the deceitfulness of riches, and the lusts of other things entering in, choke the Word, and it becometh unfruitful. And these are they which are sown on good ground; such as hear the Word, and receive it, and bring forth fruit, some thirtyfold, some sixty, and some an hundred'" (KJV).

Jesus said, "Whoever has ears to hear, let him hear." Why did He say that? Whoever has ears to hear, let him hear ... Have you ever noticed how many times the Bible refers to hearing and God it says it twice? "Faith cometh by hearing and hearing by the word of God." And "He who has ears to hear, let him hear." Listen, this is so important because Jesus goes on to explain what the parable means. "When He was alone, the twelve and the others around Him asked Him about the parables." He told them, "The secret of the Kingdom of God has been given to you, but to those on the outside, everything is said in parables so that they may ever be seeing but never perceive, that they will ever be hearing, but never understand." Otherwise, they would turn and be forgiven. He said everything that is given is given in these parables so that people can see but never get it. They can hear it, but never understand it. He said this because if they would see it and get it, if they would hear it and understand it, He said then they would repent and be saved!

135

People must see and get it, they must hear it and understand it, He said. Then that is when they are converted, right? Then He says, "Don't you understand this parable? How then will you understand any?" Then He goes on to give the parable of the farmer sowing the Word. He is telling them that some people are like seed along the path where the Word is sewn; as soon as they hear it, Satan comes and takes it away.

People know that God can heal. But immediately they think, "Then why am I still sick?" That is Satan. They have just experienced a drive-by, and they did not even see it coming.

You know God can prosper you but immediately you are thinking about that bill that you have to pay that you don't have the money for. Satan has come immediately to steal that truth. Remember it is all about influence. People understand that God can *do* but are not truly sure that God *will*.

In verse 16 the Lord says, " … are like seeds sewn on rocky places; they hear the Word and at once receive it with joy, but since they have no root, they latched only a short time." They hear the Word and they receive it with joy. I had a situation at my church with a guy who assured me he was called of God and wanted me to be his spiritual father. I shared some things with him about his behavior and what he should do and should not do. When I was preaching, he was the loudest one in the group — shouting me down. Not because he was encouraging me, but because he was bringing attention to himself. He was taking away from what God was doing. Some people are a pleasure to preach to because they are genuinely interacting, but in this situation such was not the case. This man was shoplifting the service. He was trying to steal the message. I brought correction and understanding to all that. As this portion of Scripture tells us, certain people receive the Word with joy, but they cannot stick around or stay planted! Because they cannot hold to the things of God because of offense!

Such people only last a short time in their faith. Verse 17 says, "When trouble or persecution comes because of ... they quickly fall away." One version (NLT) says, "They fall away as soon as they have problems or are persecuted for believing God's word." Satan will levy an attack against you when you are *trying* to believe the Word. When you are just trying, it becomes even harder. Listen, if you really are trying to do that, then buckle up and hold on. Get your boots and lace them puppies up straight, get your back stiffened up, square off your shoulders and realize that this is about to be on! Because the persecution will come, not because you are doing anything wrong, but because you have taken the position or the stance to believe God! And just assuming that you are "stupid" enough to believe God! I'm not talking down at you, because I am stupid enough to believe God. I take Him at his Word! So the moment you make that decision, the attack comes!

Persecution Comes Because of the Word's Sake.

Because of the Word, this type of person quickly falls away. Still others, like seed sown among thorns, hear the Word, but the worries of this life and the deceitfulness of wealth and the desire for other things come in and choke the Word, making it unfruitful. Yet others, like seed sown in good soil, hear the Word, accept it, and produce a crop. Some thirty- some sixty- and some one hundredfold from what was sown. Now, remember how I said to you that the word *offense* means "stumbling block"? An offense causes someone to trip and fall. Here in Mark 4, where Jesus says that the desires of life come in and choke out the plants that spring

137

up from the Word and then they fall away, that is the same word, *offense*. Offense comes because you may be enduring persecution because for the Word's sake. You may also be dealing with things that are coming at you from the world. The world comes and chokes out the Word. The worldly influence takes you away from the things of God; it chokes it out until you have no more breath in you. And Jesus says that the ones who hear the Word and then plant it in their heart are the ones who produce, some thirty-, some sixty-, and some one hundredfold.

There are different types of dirt. What type of dirt are you? Are you the kind who gets so excited when you hear the Word but then there is not enough substance in you so you fall away from it? Are you one of the kind that gets everything choked out of you by the world? The kind that says, "I know the Word says this, but I can't tithe because I don't have the money"? Really? That is the reason why you don't have the money. The world comes in saying, "Well, that is just unrealistic; I'm not doing that." Okay, but listen; do me a favor — if you are not going to tithe in obedience to the Word, don't call your pastor when the financial problems happen, because there is nothing the church can do for you if you won't do the Word. We don't have another gospel. We don't have another Bible. We only have one.

What type of dirt are you? That is the question you need to ask yourself. What kind of dirt am I? Am I the one that can hear the Word, receive it, put it in my heart and then do it and trust that God has got me? Or am I the one that gets offended because of the Word's sake. I want you to be successful and I want you to recognize the attempt that Satan is waging against your life, because some of us do not even realize that maybe the elephants have *not* been released in your life, but then arrows have been shot.

138

And then arrows are coming at you and you are not even paying attention. The next thing you know, you are getting hit and you are wondering why. Then the next thing you know, Satan is trying to divide and you are wondering why. This is so important! You must get this.

Chapter Seven: Responding From Your Position

John 1:17

"For the law was given by Moses, but grace and truth came by Jesus Christ" (KJV).

The law was given by Moses, and the law was written upon stone tablets. Grace and truth came through Jesus Christ. The law, which was written in the Old Testament, came by Moses, but the Bible says that grace and truth came by Jesus Christ. This tends to be a very difficult proposition, because church folks are amongst the most judgmental, hypocritical folks you shall ever find. We run up against this criticism because in today's culture and society, church people begin to evaluate the world based on the world's system. So if I am a doctor then I am considered important and my income reflects that. But if I am a teacher then I am paid way less than a doctor gets paid. But the reality is that if Americans want to have a decent future, then they had better pay teachers well enough for them to stay doing what they are doing with joy and excitement, because these are the people shaping our future generations.

The world deems success based on how much money a person makes, what type of work he or she does for a living, but the reality is that when Jesus showed up, He said, "Think not that I came to be served." He said, "I came to serve." The disciples were all fighting over who was going to be sitting next to him in heaven! Jesus let them know that the greatest shall be the least. It was a whole different thought process, a whole different system. Because the reality is, we gauge things in the world by "What do you do? Who are you? If you are important, than you are important, or you are this and that." God's system does not function that way. It never did and it never will. God's system is not about what you do, it is not about who you are; it is about *Whose* you are. This is a very different understanding of value.

As you gain understanding of God's economy, you come to a place of being able to preach grace, and people start saying, "Wait a minute, do you mean to tell me it is not about what I do?" No! It is not about what you do! But if you are saved, then you will do! The Old Testament Law was centered on the idea of "Do this to live." Then Jesus entered the scene, and now *you live to do this*. So now you live to do, not you do to live. This is a very different understanding, but there is joy in being able to serve God! There is joy in being able to worship God! There is joy in being able to know that your God, who loved you first and gave Himself for you, loved you that much, that He moved heaven and hell. He stepped off of his throne and touched the Earth just for you! Do we even understand the magnitude of that love? I ask this because most people would not do that for you. Most people would not even answer your phone call, much less step off their throne to touch this world. That is grace.

Psalms 1:1

"Blessed is the man that walketh not in the counsel of the ungodly, nor standeth in the way of sinners, nor sitteth in the seat of the scornful" (KJV).

Notice that the psalmist says, "Who walks not in the counsel of the ungodly." Whenever the Bible speaks of *walking*, it always refers to how you are living your life, or walking something out. So what the psalmist is saying is that people who live after the counsel of the ungodly are not blessed. People who stand in the way of sinners are taking a position or a stand as a sinner would take it. These people are putting themselves against God.

You have to understand that the way you stand and resist attack in your life is not as a sinner. Have you ever heard people say, "Oh, I'm just a sinner saved by grace!" Listen! You *were* a sinner, but you are no longer. Once you have accepted Jesus as your Lord and Savior, you are no longer a sinner saved by grace. You were a sinner who was saved by grace, but now you *are* the righteousness of God. You are made in His image, you have been transformed, and you have been translated from the kingdom of darkness into the Kingdom of Light!

Then the psalm goes on to say, those "who sitteth in the seat of the scornful." Have you ever watched someone who is scornful? This person is upset, bothered, scorned, and bitter. And sitting in that seat of bitterness or scorn changes every bit of your perspective. Everybody is against you, nobody likes you, everybody deserves to die and you are in a bad place. The scornful

143

person's your whole world is judged from the seat of scornful people, lifestyle and a scornful attitude. We see in Psalms 1 the following three stages: *sit, walk and stand.*

The book of Ephesians was a letter written by the Apostle Paul. Paul was in prison and he was writing to the church at Ephesus, which he founded and was at the time about three or so years old. The book of Ephesians is considered to be the blueprint of Christian maturity. If you want to understand your Christianity, just read the book of Ephesians. It is only six chapters long. If you will read it, I guarantee you, you will come to extreme revelations about who you are in Christ and what you have through Christ. The entire book of Ephesians deals with these same three subjects found in Psalms 1: sit, walk and stand. Chapters 1 through 3 deal with *how you sit positionally.*

Ephesians 1:17

"That the God of our Lord Jesus Christ, the Father of glory, may give unto you the spirit of wisdom and revelation in the knowledge of him: the eyes of your understanding being enlightened; that ye may know what is the hope of His calling, and what the riches of the glory of His inheritance in the saints, and what is the exceeding greatness of His power to us-ward who believe, according to the working of His mighty power, which He wrought in Christ, when He raised Him from the dead, and set Him at his own right hand in the heavenly places, far above all principality, and power, and might, and dominion, and every name that is named, not only in this world, but also in that which is to come."

Grace completely changes your identity. Now, Paul is very clear when he starts off the book of Ephesians, because he is talking to a fairly new church and he is helping them to understand. He is sharing with them where Christ is because Christ is not still on the cross. Contrary to what a crucifix may show you, Christ was on the cross, but He is not still on the cross. He is now seated in heavenly places, far above all principality, far above all power, far above all might, *all*. So if He is seated in heavenly places, far above all these things, then Christ is above every situation that could ever come about in this world and the one to come. So, how does it help us to know where Christ is? Because that is where He is, right?

Ephesians 2:6

"And hath raised us up together, and made us sit together in heavenly places in Christ Jesus."

So then he made us sit together with Christ. Paul has spent all this time telling you where Christ is to let you know where *you* are. Christ is seated in heavenly places.

Ephesians 6:12

"For we wrestle not against flesh and blood, but against principalities, against powers, against the rulers of the darkness of this world, against spiritual wickedness in high places."

Now the Apostle Paul begins to clarify what it is that we wrestle with in this world. And he begins to explain, if you understand the text, the hierarchy in which demonic activity and evil function. He is telling us that we do not wrestle against flesh and blood, the individual or the person who seems to be opposing us, but that we wrestle against principalities and powers. We wrestle against spiritual wickedness in heavenly places, and we wrestle against the rulers of this world. Paul is being very clear to establish where the attacks are coming from and the hierarchy associated with them.

When Paul says in 2 Corinthians 12:2-4 that he knew a man that was caught up in the third heaven, he is referring to himself. The third heaven is where God's throne is. There is nothing higher than the throne of God. Naturally if there is a third heaven, we can deduce that there are a second and first. The second heaven is a realm of spiritual activity. When Paul says "wickedness in high places," he is referring to the second heaven and the realm of spiritual activity that pervades in today's society and world. This spiritual wickedness comes down from the second heaven into the first heaven, which is the Earth's atmosphere.

Let's return to these thoughts from chapter one. You must understand the importance of why Paul said God has quickened us together and seated us with Christ in heavenly places. What the apostle was helping you to understand is that if you respond to demonic activity from flesh and blood, you are under, that is, you have to be subject to the earthly realm and its rules and laws. Remember Paul has told us that the law was not given but to remind us, or make us conscious of sin.

It is like seeing a speed limit sign while you are driving your car. Let's say the speed limit is 55 mph. That speed limit sign is not meant for you to stay focused on the sign; you are supposed to be driving. But what does the sign do? The sign makes you aware that if you drive faster than that posted limit, you are now in violation of law and it makes you mindful of what the law is! But if I am driving on the autobahn in Germany, the speed limit in Phoenix doesn't matter anymore. You must understand that what Paul is helping us to understand in this Scripture is that we have been quickened, made alive, together and that we are seated in the highest of heavenly places. If you tried to deal with Satan from a subordinate position out of the flesh and blood, you cannot handle him. Because he cannot be ordered around except but by the throne which is at the top, i.e., the third heaven and throne room of God.

Have you ever heard of the statement, "It only rolls downhill"? Spiritually Paul is establishing and setting up the order. He is helping us to know that there are rulers of darkness and rulers of this world. There are people who are ruling in this world who are demonically inspired. Do you understand that when you look at certain people in power, some of those people were demonically placed in power? They are rulers.

We have people in the first heaven, or should I say the atmosphere in this world, and then we have spiritual things in the second heaven, which are demonic activity, angels, and demons. Finally you have the throne of God in the third heaven. So when you read that we were quickened together with Christ, you need to understand that you were not asked, you were made to sit with Christ. That means that you are seated *positionally* with Jesus Christ so that when you deal with adversity, it should be dealt with from your *position*.

If I am seated in heavenly places with Christ, and I am a king, the king does not have to go to war. What the king has to do is tell his army to go to war. What the king has to do is issue a decree, and people go to war. So that is how I deal with circumstances — from my position, seated in heavenly places. I am supposed to speak to the circumstance knowing that I am not necessarily the one with the power, but I have the authority over it!

147

Remember the difference between power and authority? It is very simple. If I step out into the middle of the street and a semi truck is coming at me and I yell "Stop," and the truck driver does not see me or recognize me, or I step out too quickly, I do not have the power to stop it. But if I pull out in a police car or a helicopter with a bunch of guns, and I say "Stop!" If I am a police officer and I blow my whistle and flash my lights, that truck driver most likely is going to stop his vehicle. While I have not suddenly acquired the physical strength to stop the truck, I recognize that in this situation, I do have authority. It truly is not the police officer as a person that forces everyone to stop; it is the power behind his badge and the authority that he represents.

So in understanding your authority, you realize that what Paul was helping us to ascertain, is that you cannot exercise authority if you have not been given the right position. So if you judge yourself by the law, then you will always feel that you are inadequate. "Well I messed up." So what? "Well I made some mistakes." So what? Repent, get it under the blood of Christ, and move on. "Well, you don't know what I did." You don't know what we all have done. We could play that game all day long, but the reality is that God does not view you based on things you have done, because your position is that you are seated in heavenly places.

Ephesians 2:7-9

"That in the ages to come He might shew the exceeding riches of His grace in His kindness toward us through Christ Jesus. For by grace are ye saved through faith; and that not of yourselves: it is the gift of God: not of works, lest any man should boast" (KJV).

148

Salvation is a gift. "Not of yourselves" means that it is a free gift. "Lest any man should boast" about his own abilities. It is selfishness that causes you to begin to reflect on you, to obtain the blessing of God. It is arrogance. There is no way you could obtain the blessing of God through your own abilities, because the blessings of God come by grace. Grace is accessed through faith, but that faith comes as a gift! So if you have grace in your life, then the only way you access it is by faith, because it is given to you as a free gift.

Ephesians 1:9-11

"He made known to us the mystery of His will, according to His kind intention which He purposed in Him with a view to an administration suitable to the fullness of the times, that is, the summing up of all things in Christ, things in the heavens and things on the earth. In Him also we have obtained an inheritance, having been predestined according to His purpose who works all things after the counsel of His will" (NASB).

Verse 10 says that we see with a view to an administration, in other words, with a view to a government or kingdom. Then Paul adds that the summing up of all things in the heavens and things on Earth is in Christ. If I told you a whole story, or I gave a whole sermon and I asked you to sum it up, you would then give me what you would find to be the conclusion, or the gist of what you have understood me to have said. The sum of it would be the very bare essentials of the message. So if I was to sum something up, I would then take what is big and put it into something easily communicated, portable, and transferable. That is what I would mean if I said, "Sum it all up."

Paul is saying here that everything you do is estimated in Christ. Everything you are is estimated by Christ! Everything you will ever be is estimated by Christ! It is not evaluated by your ability! It is not evaluated by what you do! It is not evaluated by who you think you are! It is evaluated by one Person and His name is Jesus Christ; it is evaluated by Christ himself. It is summed up in Christ. He is the Author and the Finisher of our faith. He is the Alpha and the Omega. He is the First and the Last, and He is the One! But do you realize how religious people struggle with that? They want to take Christ off the throne and mitigate everything that He came to do. This is why some people will struggle thinking that Christianity has to do with a pious image or religion. It is all about relationship.

Orthodoxy and orthopraxy are two different things. To be *orthodox* is to "have the right belief system," and to be *orthoprax* is to "have the right practices." Now the challenge with religion is that religion focuses on having the right practices, and, hopefully, religious people will get a better understanding of their belief system. When the reality is, God needs you to believe right first. And out of your correct understanding will come the correct practices.

There should be a desire and a burning in you to build a life centered upon God and to want to seek after Him and to be among His people and to fellowship with His people, not because you are anything in and of yourself, but because you realize you are nothing! And you have a desire that says, "You know, I just want to be with God's people and I want to be in the ministry and I want to serve God." Not because you have to. This is where grace steps into our life. Grace is accessed by the spirit and God's Spirit in you is going to tell you, "You need to be around people who will

150

inspire your faith; you need to be around people who will feed you, and you need to be around people of your own company!" This is why ministries struggle. It is hard when you are not around people of your own kind — people who believe like you do.

Everything is summed up by Christ. You need to ask yourself, "What did Christ do when He was here on this planet?" Did He go hang out with the Sadducees and the Pharisees or did he go among the sick and impoverished? He was looking for the ones who needed Him. That is why He said the sick are the ones who need a physician.

Everything is summed up by Christ. And if you would evaluate life that way, you would make better decisions. What would Christ do? Do you think Christ would be at the movies instead of being among His people worshiping Him? I am serious! Sometimes people will take the grace teaching to an extreme and give themselves some "sloppy agape." "Well," they think, "God loves me so I can just do whatever I want to do without consequence or repercussion." God loves you so you can love, serve and worship Him, not continue in error. He loves you too much to leave you the way He found you.

"Oh, I just don't feel like it," you might say. Nobody asked you what you feel.

We put ourselves in a place where we don't understand that everything is summed up in Christ.

So verse 11 says also that we have obtained an inheritance having been *predestined*. So having been predestined — Do you ever hear somebody say, "It is my destiny"? Your life is predestinated in Christ. You do not have godly destiny outside of

Christ. You have no purpose outside of Christ. You have no value outside of Christ. But once you are "In Him," the Bible says that you have obtained an *inheritance.*

Now to have obtained an inheritance means that arrangements have been legally made in advance so that now you can receive what is being given to you, right? So if you have an inheritance, having been predestined according to His purpose and after His counsel, then whatever he has predestined for you to be and to be called to do, whatever that may be, that calling is given by God, that mission is ordained by God, and He is the One who has predestinated your life; your life is not your own. You are saved by grace through faith. By grace you are empowered to do everything that God called you to do and asked you to do! Isn't that something?

And the Word says these things are after the counsel of His will. According to His purpose. Not of you, because then you could boast. I am not smart enough to preach. I am not gifted enough; I am not eloquent enough; because it is God who allows me and enables me and graces me to do what He has called me to do. So that it is clear that it is of Him and not of me!

Listen! There is a difference between "Pastor" and "Gene." Gene you hang out with; he cuts up; anybody who has traveled with me knows I can have a time. Once the "Pastor hat" goes on, though, once the office comes on, it is a whole different world. Why? Because that is a whole different thing altogether. And knowing you have been predestinated helps you to understand that God, before the foundation of the world, knew you and had a plan for you, had a purpose for you.

People in the world struggle because they are wondering what is their purpose in life. If you want to know what to do in life then we pastors and teachers need to teach you how to get "in Him." Because from your position seated with Christ, you now can have a better bird's eye view of what is going on. There is nothing worse than someone stuck in the muck and mire trying to figure out "What is my purpose in life?" Right now your purpose is to get out of that muck, because you cannot help anybody else from that situation.

Adam was created on the sixth day. What did God do on the seventh day? Rest! I want you to think about a situation in your life where you had a project to do, somebody was supposed to help you, and then that person who was supposed to help you showed up late and all the work was done. Were you a little bothered by that? Why didn't God create man on the first day then say, "Now help me do all of this"? See, the original relationship between man and God was not to have man do it, but God said, "I am going to do it, and then I am going to allow you to benefit from what I have already done."

Listen, God had a Sabbath not because He needed one but as a demonstration to show us what to do. Did God go back to work on the eighth day? No! We don't understand rest because we cannot understand sitting. When you stand, the pressure of your body is being supported by you. If all of your muscles quit working, you would collapse. But when you sit, you are able to relax. And you understand that every part of you is being supported by the chair in which you sit. God did not bring Adam in and say, "All right Adam, listen; I want you to go ahead over there and spread that water and split it up and do that, and I am going to go over here and deal with the day and night and we'll meet back here

153

in about three hours." What did He do? He put Adam in the garden and showed him all that He had given him and told him to protect it and keep it.

Ephesians 4:1

"I therefore, the prisoner of the Lord, beseech you that ye walk worthy of the vocation wherewith ye are called."

Chapters 4-6 of Ephesians talk about the Christian's walk. In chapter 4, verse 1, does it say, "You will be called"? Or does it say, "You are called"? It is telling you to walk worthy of what you are already called to. Walk worthy of what you are already equipped for. Our lives are not lived in terms of what we do to live, but what we live to do. You were put in right standing with God; you were already called! You are already equipped; you are already empowered! If you are seated in heavenly places, then you are already set up.

So then how you live your life should be a byproduct of the Christ in you! Would God not want to be around His people? Would God not want to be in church? So then, out of your desires, would God want to hurt His fellow Christians? Would God want to hurt the work of God that He has called us to? So then you are now in the position to see things and to understand things and to discern the impact of what you do and your supply and what God has asked you for. When Paul says you are part of the body and each person has a supply to bring, then you realize and recognize your part to play! And if you would see it from God's perspective, you could not help but love! You could not help but want to be involved! You would see it from up high, seated in your heavenly position!

God does not control your mind. God does not control your body. You hear people say that God made them do it. As Dad Hagin would say, "I'd rather hear a mule braying in a tin barn than listen to that craziness!" The Bible says the spirit of the prophet is subject to the prophet.

Paul continues and lets the Ephesians know that he is a prisoner of the Lord and beseeches them to walk worthy. How do you walk worthy? If you recognize that you are of a higher status then you handle yourself differently. When you walk worthy of where you were called to, when you understand your position in Christ, you see things differently. You don't think about life in terms of just trying to get by or trying to get through the struggle.

When you are the king, whatever you are frustrated with you are able to speak and change it. If you don't like something that is being done, then you can say, "I don't want this done anymore." And that situation has to change. But see, because people have "victim" mentalities, they act like a victim. "Well, you don't understand what I'm going through," they say. "It's not that easy." It is not that easy in the flesh. But some things in your life you are going to have to take control of and take authority over them by the Spirit. You are going to have to get into your position, stop trying to be in the boiler room shoveling coal, get up out of there and get back in the cat-bird seat and then begin to speak to these things and deal with these situations in your life and watch that they will change. But they cannot change if you do not understand that your identity is different.

The final chapter, chapter 6, deals with standing.

Ephesians 6:10-14

"Finally, my brethren, be strong in the Lord, and in the power of His might. Put on the whole armor of God, that ye may be able to stand against the wiles of the devil. For we wrestle not against flesh and blood, but against principalities, against powers, against the rulers of the darkness of this world, against spiritual wickedness in high places. Wherefore take unto you the whole armor of God, that ye may be able to withstand in the evil day, and having done all, to stand. Stand therefore, having your loins girt about with truth, and having on the breastplate of righteousness" (KJV).

This portion of Scripture tells us to be strong in God's might. How are you going to have His might if you are trying to do things in your own might? We are to function in the power of His might, His strength, and His ability. When we try with our ability, our strength and anything related to us, we will not be successful. Then in verse 11 Paul says, "Put on the whole armor of God that you will..." be able to do what? Sit, walk and stand. "Firm against the schemes of the devil." The wiles of the devil — do you remember Wile E. Coyote? Wiles are plans and strategies, and Satan is always planning, he is always plotting and he is always strategizing against the plan of God. If you happen to get in the middle of that, then he will be planning and strategizing against you to get you to think incorrectly and to separate you from your supply.

The devil wants to do things to derail the plan of God in your life. Do you want to know how you can know when God's plan is being derailed? You begin to see things as futile; you begin to see things as useless; you no longer have excitement about the things of God. You no longer want to be a part of God's plan.

156

Everything else in the world takes precedence. You have lost your focus.

This is why Paul tells us that our struggle is not against flesh and blood, but against rulers, against powers, against world forces of this darkness, against the spiritual forces of wickedness in heavenly places. Ephesians chapter 6 certainly produces the imagery of putting on war paint and armor and going to battle. But how do you stand and fight at the same time? If I tell you to stand right there, and then I say, "We are all going to war," am I really telling you to go to war? What am I really telling you? If I tell you to stand right here, I am telling you to guard something.

Paul says to stand, and most people articulate that in a way that would lead you to believe that he is teaching you how to advance and how to fight against Satan, as one who is seeking to gain territory, or to gain ground. If I am in a war and I am in a battle and I am going to advance, I am going to take over countries. I am going to take over cities, and I am advancing in order to take over what now does not belong to me. When I have won the war, then it will belong to me.

If I understand that when the Bible says that the Earth is His and the fullness thereof, then am I really advancing to take over new territory, or am I really advancing to protect what belongs to me? If God has told me to stand, then He is really telling me to go, take back, and protect what already belongs to Him! Your healing already belongs to you! Your prosperity already belongs to you! He is telling you to stand, because if you would get into your position and you would get into your spot and stay there, then what you are doing is standing to protect, to keep Satan from advancing against you. That is why His Word says the gates of hell shall not prevail against my church. Because Satan is always advancing against you.

All of a sudden your favorite movie comes out on a Sunday, and you stop going to church and you have lost territory. The things of God are not so important anymore and you lose some more territory. And then you begin wondering why it feels like the grace of God is lifting in your life. You hear people say, "Oh, I am graced to deal with the kids!" and then three months later, "Oh, the grace has lifted."

Do you have grace by your own abilities? It is a free gift. So if it is a free gift, are you to lead me to believe that God came and took it back? So then if we are not operating in our grace to do what God called us to do, then what we really have is not a grace problem, we have a faith problem.

There are three laws that are written in the hearts of man. The laws that were written on the tablets of stone are the Ten Commandments. The laws that were written *in the hearts of men*, Hebrews tells us, are the *Law of Liberty*, the *Law of Love* and the *Law of Faith*. As the church, these are the laws we live by, the law of perfect liberty, the law of faith and the law of love. So here is the thing: If you lose sight of your grace, you have lost sight of your position. And if you have lost sight of your position, then you are down on the first floor trying to fight a battle that you are not capable of winning from the ground, until you elevate yourself back to your superior position in which you were seated. Then from that position far above, you speak down to these things of wickedness in heavenly places because they are under your feet!

Everything about the armor of God is based on your position first. That is why Paul has spent all this time, chapters 1-6, helping you to understand Whose you are, what your position is, how you are seated, and how to walk. Then at the very end the Apostle says, "Now, let me teach you how to fight." You fight from your position. You fight from Whose you are. You understand that if you are in Christ then you are not to be down here fighting it out with flesh and blood. You can say to the devil and his minions, "I'm not going to cut you. I 'm not going to cuss you out. What I am going to do is get away from you, and I am going to start rebuking that foul spirit that is working in you until that foul spirit breaks off of you and leaves me alone! Because that is what I am called to do; that is my position.

And the challenge is, people do not understand the connection, so they start backing away from the things of God because they are overwhelmed by their condition and have forgotten their true position. Slowly but surely, it is just a matter of time.

People relegate grace as just unmerited favor. Certainly grace is unmerited favor, but it is also empowerment. God will give you the ability to do what He has asked you to do. Do you understand that if God told me to go to do a meeting somewhere on Saturday night, and I had to fly all night to get back here for Sunday morning and my plane landed at 8:00 a.m., and I was up here in the pulpit at 9:15 a.m., exhausted and tired, do you realize that if God told me to do it, that when I step into this pulpit, the power of God would hit me so hard that I would be able to execute with precision that which He has asked me to do? How is that possible? I understand that by faith I access His grace, and if He tells me to do it then He gives me the ability to do it. The task is not of my own abilities because in the natural I would be exhausted. In the natural I would be ready to pass out.

159

The battle is in your mind. If you don't believe you can do it, if you don't have faith that you can do it, you will never do it. And how can you stand against the attack and the strategy that Satan is throwing at you if your mind is not in a heavenly place? That is why an understanding of *sit, walk, stand* is so important. Because it begins to help you to understand that by grace you were made to sit in heavenly places. By grace, you are now empowered to walk this vocation to which you were called. And then once you have done those two things, now you are able to stand. When did you take the territory? To understand the reality of standing in your battle you need to know that you are protecting territory — so when did you get the territory? Two thousand years ago when Jesus hung on the cross and said, "It is finished."

It is finished. What was He saying? The same thing God told Adam — it is done. Protect it and keep it. It is finished; it is over. He put Adam in the garden and said, "Listen, I did all the work; I got it all prepared for you; now protect it and keep it." When God is telling you to stand, after you have done all you know to do, then stand again. God is telling you to protect it and keep it! Don't you let people rob you of your grace! Don't you let people steal from you! Hold on to your grace and realize that God has given you the ability to do all things through Christ who strengthens you! But not from down here. You have got to step up. And I guarantee you if you sit where God has seated you, your perspective will change. You will go, "Oh yeah, I can do that. I see the plan; I see it now, yeah." Remember when you are down in the midst of it, it becomes hard to see clearly.

One of the biggest causes of failure for a business is working *in* it and not *on* it. The only way you can work on it is to do what they call "Get up on the balcony." It is a business

160

management term. What does getting up on the balcony mean? You have got to step up to a higher level and look down at it and see how all the pieces work together, see how everything comes together. You begin to see how this piece over here fits with that piece over there. When you get up higher, you can say from that perspective, "Oh! I get that; I see that. Oh, okay, thanks, Lord, for showing that to me." There is nothing worse than a Christian who does not know who he or she is, does not know his or her identity because of running around afraid. These poor Christians run around in fear and struggling, not knowing that all the while, they already have the territory, and because they don't know it, Satan is sneaking up behind them stealing stuff from them.

Chapter Eight: Maintaining Proper Perspective

Ephesians 6:10-14a

"Finally, my brethren, be strong in the Lord, and in the power of his might. Put on the whole armor of God, that ye may be able to stand against the wiles of the devil. For we wrestle not against flesh and blood, but against principalities, against powers, against the rulers of the darkness of this world, against spiritual wickedness in high places. Wherefore take unto you the whole armor of God, that ye may be able to withstand in the evil day, and having done all, to stand. Stand therefore."

The Bible says to be strong in the Lord and in the strength of *whose* might? "Put on the whole armor of God." Not pieces of it, but the whole armor. "That you may be able to stand against the schemes of the devil." The ESV version uses the word "schemes," the King James says, "the wiles." Wile E. Coyote from the Looney Tunes "Road Runner" cartoons was constantly trying to devise a scheme that would trap the roadrunner. *Wiles* are plans, strategies and pursuits.

Now clearly, we wrestle not against flesh and blood, but we wrestle against principalities and powers. We must also come to the clarity that we are not wrestling against people, we are not wrestling against things; we are wrestling against an institution that has been established and a kingdom that has been established on this planet Earth that is run by its god, which is Satan. I don't think we realize that God is a just God and in God there is no wavering.

God is equally as just to Satan as He is to us. People often misunderstand that Satan has a lease on this planet and a right to be here. The Bible tells us that it rains on the just and the unjust. Sometimes people justify their ill treatment of others by saying, "Well this person is not right." So they treat these people differently under the premise that they are not right anyway.

But the reality is, if you are a holy and just God then you are no respecter of persons and have no ability to waver. If God promised Satan that he can have rights on this Earth for a period of time, then guess what? God will never take those rights from the devil no matter how much you cry. Crying does not move the hand of God. If a need moved the hand of God, there would be no poverty in this world. There are plenty of people who have needs, but need does not activate the power of God. Faith does!

What Is Spiritual Warfare?

Let me say it this way: There is a lot of error in terms of spiritual warfare being taught in the church today. People are battling; I do not know what they are battling. The Bible that I have tells me that Jesus has already defeated Satan. So therefore, I am not warring against Satan, I am walking in what Jesus has already done for me. I understand that I wrestle. The Apostle Paul did not say we *war* against principalities and powers, he said we *wrestle*.

So you may be wrestling. Let's say you have a thought process that you are wrestling with. You are wavering back and forth; that is really what you are doing. We do not wrestle against flesh and blood, but we are wrestling with principalities and powers — it is *not* that you are *warring* against them; it is that you must be walking in the truth of Christ's victory and you must stay walking in it. Because if you are wavering back and forth — if one day you are on this side and the next day you are on that side because your emotions have moved you — then you are wrestling.

So if we are wrestling against principalities and powers, then we have to know that in order to conquer that wrestling process, we must stand.

2 Corinthians 2:11

"Lest Satan should get an advantage of us: for we are not ignorant of his devices."

Most Christians think Satan is looking for them personally or he is looking for their possessions. That is not altogether true. Satan does seek advantage in your life. Did you hear me? The thing that Satan seeks for in your life is not your possessions; it is really not you — it is advantage over you.

Satan seeks to have advantage over us. And the only way that Satan can move in the Christian's life is to have an advantage. I think one of the challenges that people face in today's Christianity is that no one is teaching how to be righteous and holy and how to live in accordance with the way that God has told us to live. The majority of what Christians go through that feels like spiritual attack is really not an attack from Satan; it is more a cause of or a response to our behavior.

Most of us would love to blame what we go through on someone else, would love to blame it on Satan, would love to blame it on whatever. Sometimes it is just "stinkin' thinkin'." Some of it is bad behavior. Some of it is just flat out stupidity. And the reality is when you tell that to people, they become upset that it might be their fault.

Let me put it this way: Not everything in your life is your fault. There are some things that come into your life to check you, just to see where you truly stand. Have you ever cut open a piece of chicken and it is still raw in the middle? It is one of the worst things in the world. Sometimes events happen just to make sure you are *done* all the way through.

You cannot be ignorant of Satan's devices. The same word that is used for *devices* is also used to mean *strategies*. Paul is referring to the *wiles* of the devil, the *strategies* of the devil, the *plans* of the devil. What he is saying is, "I am not going to give him an advantage because I am not oblivious to his devices." And the reality is his devices never change; they are the same thing over and over again. In those days, it might have been wine used to excess. These days, people still struggle with alcohol and drugs. In those days, what took out Sampson was Delilah. In today's day and age, what takes out strong men of God is still Delilah! What took out Ahab was Jezebel, and Jezebel is still doing it.

If we want to walk in victory and success, we must understand that not every struggle is you "warring." I see people warring all the time. They say, "Well, pastor, I'm just warring in the spirit." Warring against whom? Warring against what? Because to me, all you are doing is stirring up the flesh.

Notice that Paul said, "I'm not ignorant of his devices because I'm not going to let him have the advantage." Now, may I ask you a question? If you and I were competing in a boxing match, and I told you, "I am going to tie one of your arms behind your back, and that is how you have to fight me," would I have an advantage? Is it likely you would lose? Probably, yes, unless you are highly skilled with that one arm!

But here is what I want you to understand: Once Satan has bound one of your arms behind your back, sometimes both of them, you will step into a battle for which you are ill equipped. That is why Paul said, "Put on the whole armor of God." Because when you put on the whole armor of God, you are loosed from the things that try to hold you back. You are loosed from the pain and the problems from the past. You are loosed from improper doctrine. You are loosed from not having faith. You are loosed from all the things that try to come upon you to keep you from adequately walking in that which God has already given you.

The reality is that people struggle with this concept of spiritual warfare because they say, "Well, you mean to tell me that it's already done?" My Bible says God has blessed me with all spiritual blessing and that I am seated with Christ in heavenly places far above principalities, far above all high places, far above addiction, far above bondage, far above fear, far above poverty, far above lack, far above sickness and disease, far above all these bits of stinkin' thinkin', far above my flesh, far above my feelings. I have been seated in Christ!

That means I have to deal with my situation not from my *condition* but from my *position*. Most people want to fight out of their condition. "Well, you know I don't have this, or I'm struggling with that, or I wish I had ... shoulda, coulda, woulda, hada ... " They are responding from their condition, not their position.

Satan's condition that he puts in your life is to put you at a disadvantage. It is to make you forget about your position. When a condition comes, all it is designed to do is to get you to forget about who you really are. If you forget who you are, then you are in a condition; and in order to remain in that condition you are forced to vacate your position.

When the apostle says, "After having done all, stand," and, "stand therefore," he is telling us that we have to realize that Christ has already defeated Satan. And Luke 19:13 says that He called ten of his servants and delivered them ten pounds and said to them, "Occupy until I come."

What does it mean to occupy? If I am a king, and I take over a territory, if I fight a war and expand my borders into a territory, I want my people to settle down in that land. Jesus did not say, "Fight until I come." He said, "Occupy." So once I have advanced into a territory, what I will do is leave a remnant force that will not fight for the territory, but will protect and defend that territory to keep hold of it, subdue it and make sure all of its resources become my kingdom's resources.

So it is not my total force the enemy is fighting; it is a remnant left over that is no longer trying to conquer territory; it is trying to hold on to territory. Therefore when the nobleman in the story says, "Occupy," he does not mean, "Go fight battles." He said, "Occupy." After you have done all to stand, stand therefore! Not in order to go forward to take territory, but at a minimum do not let Satan take back the territory that Jesus has already given you!

You are to occupy until He comes back! And when He comes back, He is coming back to see, did you hold on to it? Or did you give it to Satan because you were afraid? One translation actually says that to occupy is to do business. That means to use what you have and conduct kingdom business until Christ returns.

You are not the sick looking to be healed, you are the healed whom Satan is trying to make sick. By occupying until He comes, you do God's business by holding on to your territory. David said in Psalm 62, "I shall not be greatly moved." few verses later, he said, "I shall not be moved at all!" There is a point where you have got to understand that in the situations you may go through, God is not telling you to go charging into war, he is telling you, "Hold on to what I've given you." If you would just stand when all the hellish situation is coming at you, all you have got to do is stand. Stand — occupy until He comes.

What has Satan stolen from you? Is this situation in your life an attack from Satan? If you beat the bush long enough, Satan comes out. But you have to ask something: Is what you are going through something that you have given to Satan? Did you let him have it? If he seeks advantage and you have allowed him to have advantage over you, then realistically speaking you have given it to him.

Now, here is the beautiful part about it. Even if you have given it to him, you can take it back. Even if you did it accidentally, even if you didn't know better, if your neighbor has your lawn mower, it is time to go over there and do what? Take it back. Because the rightful owner is you!

Do you understand how this concept flies in the face of those who are "warring" in the spirit? Now please understand that I am not knocking intercession and prayer. The church desperately needs intercessors. But some people seem to think, "Well I'm just warring against Satan." Why? He is already done; it's over, it's finished. Jesus hung on the cross, and He said what? "It is finished!" Satan has already been whooped. I am not asking him, "Can I please have my stuff back?" I am telling him to give me my stuff back, not now, but *right* now!

There is a principle here that might seem to be semantics to certain people, but I assure you it is not semantics. If your mind does not think this way, then your faith is not placed in the right perspective. Occupy! Hold on!

Some people have gone through situations and now they are struggling with themselves. Let's say it's in the area of their finances, and they wonder, "Well God, I've been tithing, but You haven't financially blessed me, and I've been tithing and tithing and tithing and it doesn't work."

The devil is a liar. I said the devil is a liar! There is nothing you could do for God that he will not respond to. He is the same yesterday, today and forever. So let me just ask you this: If they tithed in the Old Testament and God blessed it, and He is the same yesterday, today and forever, how much more shall He bless tithing with a *better* covenant based on *better* promises.

Single people will sometimes say, "I've been waiting for Mr. or Mrs. Right to come." And you wind up settling for Mr. or

Mrs. Right Now. They get impatient and say, "Well, I've been waiting for God, and He ain't bringing nobody." Did you ever stop and think that maybe He loves them just as much as He loves you? And He loves them enough not to give them you yet.

The reality is, as you struggle in your heart, you begin to move away from occupying because all Satan is trying to do is move you away from the territory you have gained. When you come to the knowledge and understanding, for example, that God literally blesses the generous and not the hand of the stingy, their world gets smaller and smaller. If you begin to get a revelation of that, then all of a sudden Satan comes against it; you have gained ground. Then Satan says, "No, I can't let them think like that, because if they think like that, they might turn into generous people. If they think like that, they might actually give more than just a tithe! They might actually trust God with their finances! They might actually trust God with their life, and what will happen if they start trusting God with all those things? I am not going to let that happen!"

So immediately Satan comes to steal the ground you have gained! So we begin in our hearts to start to concern ourselves with the affairs of the world, not realizing that God has a plan. And when God has a plan for your life, He has already given it to you through the Word of God. And when you have taken a hold of something ... let me give you an example.

Remember where the Bible says, "Receive ye the Holy Ghost"? That word "receive" is LAMBANO, and it means not just to be a recipient of, but beyond that to "take hold of." You must realize that you have got to take hold of it! Whatever God has given you, you have got to take hold of it! You cannot just wait for it to come into you.

Faith *comes* by hearing, but faith is *not activated* by hearing! You can know what is right yet not do what is right! And if you know it and do not do it, the Bible says to him it is sin! We need to understand who we are positionally, and we understand that it is not about a war. It is the rest of faith.

I do not have to war. There are times where Satan will rear his head; I will deal with him. But if he does not rear his head, I do not need to deal with him. He can run around doing whatever he wants to do, as long as he does not touch this church, he does not touch our people, he does not touch my finances, he does not touch my family, he does not touch my house — he can do whatever he wants to do. He can stand outside of the window and make faces at me, but as long as he stays out there in check, then I understand that this territory belongs to me! As long as he does not cross over into my territory, he can stay there as long as he wants to. But he cannot cross this line, because having done all I know to do, the only thing left to do is to *stand*.

The Apostle Paul did not say "fight," he did not say "swing," he said "stand." You have got to get this. Because the reality is that after having done all you know to do, you must stand!

Some of you are in that position where you have done everything you were supposed to do. Then guess what? Stand — that's it! You might ask me, "Well, do you mean patience?" Yes. Patience! We live in a microwave generation where everybody wants everything now! There is no patience in today's society.

People think, "If I can't get it in two minutes and 15 seconds, I don't want it!" When the reality is what? Patience!

When you look at the story of the tortoise and the hare, the race went to the one who endured. Not to the one who moved the fastest. People get into church or ministry, and they are excited about it. But the ones who are the most excited are like firecrackers! They pop and they're done. Then you wonder, "What happened to them?" They were out there running with everything they had, not knowing where they were going and not understanding how to stand! And the moment Satan tripped them because they were running so fast, they fell flat on their face. Then they were left wondering, "What happened?" The problem is, they would not stand.

2 Corinthians 10:3-6

"For though we walk in the flesh, we do not war after the flesh: (For the weapons of our warfare are not carnal, but mighty through God to the pulling down of strong holds;) casting down imaginations, and every high thing that exalteth itself against the knowledge of God, and bringing into captivity every thought to the obedience of Christ; and having a readiness to revenge all disobedience, when your obedience is fulfilled" (KJV).

If Satan can get an advantage in our lives, then we must understand that the place where his advantage lies is in our imaginations. Because the Word says the weapons of our warfare are not carnal but mighty through God to the pulling down of strongholds. Then he begins to explain what the stronghold is; casting down all imaginations that exalt themselves against the knowledge of God. What does that mean?

173

Here is an example: The Bible tells us to go to church. "Well, I don't have to go, I'm not going ... da-da-da-da ..." Really? That attitude is a stronghold. That is exalting oneself above what God has said.

Here is another: You need to love your neighbor. "Well, they did me wrong!" That is a stronghold that has exalted itself against what God has said. And so the Apostle said the weapons of our warfare are not carnal, but mighty through God to the pulling down of strongholds.

Your battle and your warfare are not with tangible worldly things; your battle and warfare are in your mind. Your battle is casting down imaginations; it is getting rid of your attitudes; it is getting rid of your opinion. When you constantly say, "I," there is a point at which "I" has to die and has got to become, "Lord, You! What do You want? What is Your will? Your way?" That is when you cast down all imaginations, that is when you exalt the Word of God above your opinion. That is where people struggle.

People tend to not want to be told what to do. Independence is great to a point, but there will come a moment where you will not be doing what you want to do, and you will be *snap, crackle, pop* and then *sizzle*! The reality is, I am not going to trade my eternity to burn in hell because I could not get my mind around what God told me to do. In my opinion, He has made it plain; He has made it clear. I am going to live life God's way. And when I do life God's way, I get God's result!

Most people do not even think that way anymore. The world has moved into the place where they want to do what they want to do. And God's Word becomes secondary, and now knowledge has exalted itself against what? The knowledge of God!

So now our society has schools with no God in them. Now our society has courts with no God in them. Now our country has states with no God in them. Now our world has countries with no God in them. Now we have churches with no God in them. Their god has become self-help. Books are written about the five keys to a better you!

Let me give you the one key to a better life — it is called the Word of God; that is all you need. Jesus said, "The keys are given to me." He said, "And I give them to you." The church needs to take it right back to the basics. The weapons of our warfare, the true battle, are in your head. And if you cannot think it, you cannot conceive it, you cannot achieve it. It is not possible, because if you have fifty-cent conceptualizations, if you have two-cent understanding, you will have fifty-two cent manifestations. Your manifestations will never exceed your revelation. 3 John 2 says, "Beloved, above all else I wish that you will prosper and be in good health even as your soul prospers." Your soul must prosper; your soul must grow and develop.

The battle is over your soul. That is why Satan seeks to steal, kill and destroy. How do you think he gets his advantage? In your soul — mind, will and emotions.

There has to be balance. You have to understand that yes, you have authority; yes, you have the name of Jesus; yes, you have been given all power; but you must also understand that now you have to walk in these things with the right mindset!

Jesus went to pray for the madman of Gadara, and as soon as the demons saw Jesus, they were thinking, "Jesus, have you come to deal with us before our time? Wait a minute, we know who Jesus is." The madman of Gadara never saw Jesus before, so who was speaking through him? Devils! And they literally said, "Have you come to deal with us before our time?" They recognized that a time is set for them when they will eventually be dealt with. Until then, there is nothing you can do to remove them completely. Their primary purpose is to release their oppression on the world. They have a right to run around and wreak havoc in this world and not just on you!

I have heard people say that they took care of that devil and cast him into the ... whatever. No, they did not. If Jesus could not do it permanently, neither can you. Jesus cast them into pigs! It was not their time! Jesus did not say, "I came to bring an end to you permanently. I came to get you off my people!" So, Jesus laid hands on him and He said, "Who are you?" Then the man said, "We are Legion for we are many." Jesus said, "Well, thanks for sharing that information with me; now get your many butts out of here, all of you."

That is the authority. But you must understand — Jesus knew because the madman was clothed in his right mind. That is why the Bible says, "Have on the mind of Christ." Then it says later, that the madman of Gadara was sitting there off to the side "in his right mind." See, some of the situations you battle with occur because you are not in your right mind! Because if you would let the mind of Christ be in you, you would see it the way Christ sees it, you would do it the way Christ does it! It is very simple; when you see the way Christ sees, you will do what Christ does! But it is a battle that happens in the mind. You have really just got to stand. Because if you are honest, you will admit that most offense comes from anxiousness to have something that you are not ready to have.

176

1 Timothy 1:18

"This charge I commit unto thee, son Timothy, according to the prophecies which went before on thee, that thou by them mightest war a good warfare; holding faith, and a good conscience; which some having put away concerning faith have made shipwreck."

This is Paul speaking to Timothy, giving him instructions, saying, "This charge. ..." In other words, this *command.* "I commit unto you, my son Timothy. According to the prophesies which went before on thee, that thou by them mightest war a good warfare." He is telling Timothy, that, according to the prophesies which were spoken about him and before him, and the things he is about to go into, Paul warns him ahead of time how he might fight or war a good warfare.

"Wait a minute!" you are probably saying, "I thought you just said that we don't fight according to those things!" Then verse 19 says, "Let me show you how you fight the warfare. Holding faith and a good conscience, which some having put away concerning faith have made shipwreck." What is the Word telling you? Hold on to your faith and your conscience. Because some have put them away, and when they put away their conscience, they have become shipwrecked.

He did not say, "Use authority." He did not say, "Go into battle." He said, "Hold your faith and keep your conscience." Why is that important? Because some people will do stuff to you and have no conscience about it. And then after they have offended you they will think, "Well I'll just put it under the blood of Jesus," and forget all about the hurt and damage they have caused. We all have the blood of Jesus, but that does not mean you are keeping your conscience right. Because what is your conscience designed to do? To keep you walking the right way. To keep you walking in love, to keep you doing things that you should be doing. And your conscience, or the voice of the Spirit, will begin to tell you when you are not doing what is right.

But Paul warns Timothy and us that if you put that conscience away, it is a shipwreck looking for a place to happen. Notice, if you put away your conscience, you cannot fight. Oh my goodness, it is so important that Christians understand this, because you cannot live any old kind of way, you cannot act any old kind of way, you cannot go into this world any old kind of way because when you do, you are going with a disadvantage. You are going into the battle with your arm tied behind your back. And then you wonder why you are getting whooped! It stems back to, "Can you walk in love?" Can you do what is right? Are you out there acting like the world, or are you coming out and being separate from the world?

2 Timothy 2:3-5 (KJV)

"Thou therefore endure hardness, as a good soldier of Jesus Christ. No man that warreth entangleth himself with the affairs of this life; that he may please him who hath chosen him to be a soldier. And if a man also strive for masteries, yet is he not crowned, except he strive lawfully."

"Endure hardness as a good soldier of Jesus Christ." Are you ready? "No man that wars and entangles himself with the affairs of this life, that he may please Him who has chosen him to be a soldier. And if a man also strives for masteries yet he is not crowned, except he does it lawfully." In other words, no man who has been called to war gets involved with the nonsense of life. The only thing a soldier should be concerned about is pleasing the one who chose him to be a soldier. And because of that, if he is not crowned, it will be because he did not do it according to the rules.

But if we strive not to please people in this life, but to go after living the way God has told us, then we are doing it lawfully and we receive crowns.

So Paul is saying no man who goes to war entangles himself with the affairs of life. Can you imagine some soldier over in a foreign country at war with his baby in a sling on his back? Trying to fight as a soldier and take care of a child at the same time? No man who goes to war entangles himself with the nonsense of this world! But why is it that people are constantly entangling themselves with the things of the world? "Well pastor, you know we still got to live." Really? Because I died a long time ago.

That is the problem; I am not *trying* to live! It is Christ that liveth in me, for the life I live after the flesh, I now live by the Son of God who loved me and gave Himself for me! Every person who seeks his life shall lose his life. See, you have got to understand that our war is not the way people purport spiritual warfare. We do not entangle ourselves with this stuff. What are we about? The Father's business. What is the Father's business? Seek and save that which is lost. Help people move from the kingdom of darkness into the kingdom of light — that is it!

I do the best I can to cut off nonsense pretty quickly. I do not entangle myself with the stuff of life; I don't need that stuff. What do I need? More Jesus. What do I need? More God. What do I need? That the eyes of my understanding may be enlightened and I may know the hope of His calling and the riches of His inherited grace. That is what I need, that's it! That I might be filled with all the fullness of God. I do not need anything else, everything else shall come.

Who goes to war at his own expense, the Bible says. Who? Who builds a field and does not eat from it? God promised us! God promised me that if I would go into the battle not concerning yourself with the nonsense of life, and stay focused on Him, He will take care of the rest!

Matthew 6:33 says to seek first the Kingdom of God and His righteousness and all these things will be added to us. Sometimes we get crossed in our head and start thinking we have to fend for ourselves. No, we don't. Why? Because no man goes to war at his own expense. Some people are fighting and it is costing them everything! Sometimes if it seems to be costing you everything, you may be going at your own expense! And you need to step back and realize that greater is He that is in you than he that is in the world!

While I certainly do not agree with all his doctrine, this quote by Scottish theologian William Barclay truly brings greater light: "Endurance is not just the ability to bear a hard thing, but to turn it into glory." The Bible exhorts us that after having done all to stand ... stand — knowing and confident in your victory. It does not say, having done all to stand, and complain. I didn't get what I wanted so I'll just complain about it. No! He said, having done all to stand ... having your loins girded about with the truth, having your helmet of salvation on, knowing that you are saved, protect your mind. Having your shield of faith, knowing that faith will protect you. Having your sword of the spirit, knowing with confidence that you are able to speak out of your mouth and know that everything you speak that lines up with the Word of God shall come to pass! Having your breastplate of righteousness protecting your heart, knowing that you are not righteous because of you, but you are righteous because of Him!

Romans 5:1-6

"Therefore being justified by faith, we have peace with God through our Lord Jesus Christ: by whom also we have access by faith into this grace wherein we stand, and rejoice in hope of the glory of God. And not only so, but we glory in tribulations also: knowing that tribulation worketh patience; and patience, experience; and experience, hope: and hope maketh not ashamed; because the love of God is shed abroad in our hearts by the Holy Ghost which is given unto us" (KJV).

Hope will never leave us ashamed. We must understand that we have access to this grace by faith! And when we are in faith, we have the ability to endure and to stand! And do not let Satan take not one inch from you. It is *through grace* that you *access your grace* by faith. And then you understand that that is how you are able to stand.

And having done all to stand, stand some more. When you have done all you need and know to do, stand! Satan is throwing everything at you — stand! In an earlier chapter, I mentioned the ancient practice of releasing elephants as a final act of warfare. The reason the attackers did not send in the elephants first is because the elephants could destroy everything. The goal of war is not necessarily to destroy everything, but to take it over.

Satan's first plan for your life was to hurt you just enough to take everything from you. He was not trying to kill you; he was trying to take you to the brink! So now, you wonder, "Wait a minute, what's going on?" You must stand. And now that you have done all you know to do, you need to ask yourself, "Is there somebody I need to forgive? Is there something I need to do? Do I need to be involved? Do I need to give? Is there something that I need to be doing?" But once you have done all you know to do, then what you have got to do is stand.

And when the situations are flying at you from every which direction, you have got to be able to say, "Devil I am standing." The devil may try to convince you that you are about to be sick! Your Bible tells you that you are healed by the stripes of Jesus. He sent His Word and He healed you! He is the God who takes sickness out of the midst of you! You may struggle in your finances. You must remind yourself that the Bible tells us that above all else He wishes that you would prosper and be in good health even as your soul prospers.

The Lord makes rich and He adds no sorrow to it. That is how we stand. We must learn to answer all doubt and unbelief. And now when you are answering correctly then you are standing. Satan may try to come against your relationships. Let him know that God promised Abraham that He would protect his finances, He would preserve his family, He would preserve his relationships, He would provide his finances, and since you are a child of Abraham, you are the seed of Abraham, that because Jesus died on the cross that He has made you a joint heir with Abraham. You are Abraham's seed now, standing.

And when things are coming at you, you have got to learn how to stand. You cannot back up one inch because that is your territory. You have got to learn how to occupy, you have got to get to the point where it is so deep in you that you can say, "You know what, devil, I am going to occupy this space that God gave me. I am going to occupy this revelation God gave me. I am going to occupy this thing, I am not going to let go; I am not going to shrink back; I am not going to give up. This is where I am standing. I am going to stand, and when you have thrown everything at me, when you have released the elephants, I am still going to stand. Do you want to know why? Because those creatures are going to come at me, but they will stop right here! Why? Because of Christ in me, the hope of glory!" Having done all you know to do, stand!

Welcome to the Teaching Ministry of Rev. Gene Herndon, Senior Pastor of Stonepoint Community Church! For almost ten years, he has been providing simple, practical teaching and understanding of the Bible.

Our mission is to inspire, improve and help you shape your future into nothing short of the best of what God has for you! Gene Herndon Ministries is committed to bringing the truth of God's word to you in an authentic, practical, humorous and easy to apply way.

We believe that this resource will be a blessing to you. Should you like to see other resources that are available or to book Pastor Gene for any speaking engagements, please visit us on the web at www.inhimpotential.org

Other Featured Titles

Betrayal - Learning To Trust Again

Betrayal is the breaking of trust and confidence. Betrayal is often the focal point of a good movie or book but in real life it can be devastating. Not only in terms of personal relationships, friendships, and marriages but also by the church. This book will help you to begin the healing process and to quickly create healthy boundaries in your life.

$9.99 (One Book)

Getting Out of the Wilderness

God has given us many promises and the Bible tells us that the promises of God are Yes and Amen! This powerful book reveals the limiting thoughts, beliefs, and ideas that keep the believer from possessing whatever God has promised you. You will be forced to face your fears and stretch the limits set by your self imposed boundaries. This book will help you to acquire new insight to rid our-selves of the subtleties of poverty thinking that can hinder and often destroy the prosperity of God in our lives.

$9.99 (One Book)

And remember, in all you're getting, get understanding!

Made in the
USA
Lexington, KY